Building Resilience

at work

Kathryn McEwen

www.
AUSTRALIANACADEMICPRESS
.com.au

First published in 2011
Australian Academic Press
32 Jeays Street
Bowen Hills Qld 4006
Australia
www.australianacademicpress.com.au

National Library of Australia Cataloguing-in-Publication entry:

Author:	McEwen, Kathryn.
Title:	Building resilience at work / Kathryn McEwen.
ISBN:	9781921513831 (pbk.)
	9781921513848 (ebook)
Subjects:	Resilience (Personality trait)
	Self-actualization (Psychology)
	Work--Psychological aspects.

Dewey Number: 158.1

Contents

Acknowledgments

Thank you to Sonya Vandergoot and Wendy Green, who helped research the literature on resilience. My appreciation also to Spencer Briggs who read earlier drafts and diplomatically steered me in the right direction; and to my colleague and good friend Jacky Dakin, with whom I have trialled many of the activities and ideas explored here. Finally, a heartfelt thanks to my husband Allan for supporting me in my work despite a resilience journey of his own, and to our resilient sons Allan and Aled for being there with us and for us.

Exploring resilience: Understanding the journey

It is not the strongest of the species that survives, nor the most intelligent that survives. It is the one that is the most adaptable to change.

Charles Darwin

We live in a fast-paced and rapidly changing world where resilience is critical. While Charles Darwin highlighted long ago that survival of a species depends on successfully adapting to changing environments, the complexity of surviving life today adds quite a different dimension to what this means.

Why do we need to be resilient?

Despite more affluence and higher standards of living in Australia, the statistics suggest we are much less able to cope with daily life. One in five of us will experience some form of mental illness each year and annually 80,000 Australians will suffer depression. Even more worrying is the trend for more young people to be affected, with at least one third having an episode of mental illness before the age of 25.[1] It seems we live in an increasingly negative world, where younger generations are more anxious and pessimistic than their grandparents despite on the surface being better off.

In our workplaces, personal stress levels are on the increase, with higher workloads, decreased budgets, and changing demands as the organisations we work for try to respond and adapt to global competitive markets, as well as the rapidly chan   ging social, technological and climatic environment.

Workplaces, like communities, need individuals, leaders and teams who are able to survive and even thrive in the face of these challenges. We need resilience, and the good news is that we can develop and build this. This book explores how.

What is resilience?

Success is going from failure to failure without losing enthusiasm.

Sir Winston Churchill

Resilience is a complex concept with numerous definitions. Central to most of these is the notion that resilience involves being able to withstand or overcome adversity and unpleasant events and successfully adapt to change and uncertainty.

The words 'bounce-back', 'rebound' and 'recoil' are frequently used to describe how resilient people respond to setbacks and obstacles in their lives. Interestingly, the term itself is derived from the Latin word *re-salire*, which means 'jump'.

Bounce-back also incorporates some sense of personal growth as we use each adverse experience not just to enhance our coping but also to better manage the next one. In essence each event provides us an opportunity to learn new skills and anticipate, plan for, and better manage the next situation we encounter.

The upshot of all this is that resilience can only be developed when we actually experience setbacks and obstacles and work through them. Avoiding or being protected from problems is not useful and can even be detrimental to our coping ability. This is a valuable message for parents as a world of 'stranger danger' and fears for our children have created a 'bubble-wrap' generation in which managing adversity is declining at a time when it's needed most.

What makes a resilient person?

What makes us resilient? Is it an aspect of personality that we are born with or can we promote and develop it?

Many of the studies into resilience have focused on how people face physical illness or respond to disasters, stressful situations or major life changes. As our knowledge has developed, what has become clear is that resilience is not just genetic but an intertwining of personal characteristics with environmental factors. It seems we are born with a level of inbuilt resilience but how we build on this depends on our life's circumstances and responses. US studies indicate that as much as 40% of our mental wellbeing could be a factor of our outlook and activities.

On a personal level, characteristics such as optimism, flexibility, adaptability, independence and effective problem-solving skills assist us to build resilience. Social skills and a strong sense of trust in others are also beneficial, together with self-control and the capacity to suppress personal emotions and needs. If you have a sense of humour and some creativity that also helps. You are also more likely to have bounce-back ability if you have good levels of self-esteem and what psychologists call self-efficacy — the belief in your ability to succeed in particular situations.

After many years of research into personality we know that approximately 50% of personality is genetic. Don't give up yet though, as if you are not blessed with resilient qualities you can foster and develop many of them. It is possible, for example, to learn to become more optimistic, to control your emotions and problem-solve more effectively. You can also lighten up, be more flexible and improve your social skills. The baseline we start from may differ but we all have scope to raise the bar. While our personality predisposes us to behave in a certain way we can learn to adapt to the situations in which we find ourselves and shape the outcomes.

At the other end of the genetic spectrum, being born with bounce-back qualities may not suffice as resilience levels are also a product of our environment. If we have strong support from caring family, friends and workmates, as well as actively engage in activities with others, this promotes resilience. Positive and affirming — rather than negative — environments are also valuable, as are relationships that create trust and offer encouragement. The implications of these factors for workplaces are far-reaching and are explored in this book.

At a work-team level the concept of resilience has similarities with individual resilience. It is the capacity of the group to rebound from setbacks, change, pressure and conflict and develop greater effectiveness as a result of the experience. Resilient teams, like people, can be described as having characteristics such as flexibility, adaptability, a sense of fun, support, and good problem-solving skills.

Interestingly, team resilience is not the sum of each member's resilience, and emphasis needs to be placed on creating work climates that foster bounce-back. A team of resilient people does not necessarily make a resilient team in the same way that a team of champions is not a champion team. The interplay of individual and environmental factors is critical as even if we are highly resilient we can fall over in a team with negative relationships and no support or shared direction. On the other hand, using joint coping strategies in a team can increase effectiveness as members learn from each other and build on successes.

A developmental model for building resilience

This book is designed around the developmental model of resilience shown in Figure 1. It focuses on investing in the mind,

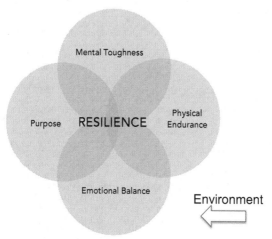

Figure 1
A developmental model of resilience.[2]

body, heart and soul, requiring you to reflect on four fundamental questions:

Mental toughness: Do you have the right mindset to address the daily challenges you face?

Physical endurance: Do you invest in your body what you expect to get out of it?

Emotional balance: Do you channel and use your emotional energy positively?

Purpose: Do you have a sense of meaning and connectiveness in what you do?

As you can see, these challenges, while posed to you personally, can equally be asked of a work team.

The theory underlying this model is that in order to develop rebound ability we need to invest in each of the four described areas. While this does not mean equal investment in each quadrant, we need to attend to each component in order to build the resilience we need for all of life's challenges.

For example, while you may need high levels of physical endurance when working long hours, it is emotional resilience that equips you for emotionally demanding events such as conflict with your colleagues. Similarly, you may be mentally tough enough to persist towards long-range goals, but it is a sense of higher meaning and purpose that makes this satisfying and worthwhile rather than stressful. A difficult day can become satisfying if you connect it to a larger sense of accomplishment.

A good analogy is running a marathon or competing in endurance sports. Successful athletes need as much mental toughness as physical fitness, as well as the ability to manage the emotional highs and lows of a gruelling event. Added to this is often a personal meaning behind competing, such as the exhilaration of running for a charitable cause, overcoming a personal disability or representing a school, community or even a country.

As you work through this book, identify which aspects of resilience come more naturally to you and are already intuitive or part of your make-up. Notice the areas where there would be benefit in investing more time and energy. Not all of the ideas and strategies will appeal to you so you will need to select and put effort into those that you believe will work for your circumstances and make-up. You can also encourage colleagues to assess themselves and the team against each of these areas.

Elements of the resilience model

So what do each of the elements of the model mean? Here is an overview.

Mental toughness. Think about somebody you think of as mentally strong. Chances are you will describe them as adaptable, confident and seemingly in control of what is happening around them. They are probably optimistic, positive and certain of their strengths and ability to succeed in specific situations. Chapters 2 and 3 offer details on how to develop this mental or cognitive aspect of resilience.

Physical endurance. Physical endurance emphasises the need to care for our bodies in the way that we know we should, but don't always do. It incorporates exercise, good nutrition and working with our body rhythms. Understanding our body's early warning system and ensuring self-care all helps us develop physical strength, flexibility and endurance. This does not necessarily mean being super fit, rather being physically able to do what we need to do on a day-to-day basis. This of course varies from person to person. Chapters 4 and 5 provide useful ideas on how to develop this physical hardiness, especially in relation to our working life.

Emotional balance. Do you have emotional balance? To be emotionally resilient we need to be both aware of and accepting of our feelings and able to develop and maintain effective relationships with others. We also need to be able to manage negative feelings, which means a certain degree of emotional control and suppression of our own needs in particular situations. People strong in this characteristic create positive energy around them and are keen to give and receive support. Ways in which you can build your emotional resilience are detailed in Chapters 6 and 7.

Purpose and meaning. A less-recognised aspect of resilience, purpose, recognises our need as human beings to have meaning in our lives and a sense of connection with our community and the world at large. Investment in this area involves living authentically by being true to ourselves and acting in ways consistent with our underlying values and beliefs. Having a balanced life by spending time on the things that matter is also an integral aspect of this. If you would like to understand more about this area then Chapters 8 and 9 provide plenty of tips.

How to get the most out of this book

The following chapters explore how you can build your personal resilience at work and better deal with the pressures you face. It focuses on daily challenges and is not meant as advice for dealing with trauma, diagnosed mental illness or major difficulties, all of which may require professional support.

It is best to consider resilience as a preventative strategy, a sort of protective mechanism that better equips you to deal with difficulties when they eventuate.

The information presented is not 'pop psychology' but is based on models and theories from psychological research; in particular, from the positive psychology movement also known as the science of the good life. In contrast to a traditional focus on mental illness, positive psychologists explore how to help the average 'well' person become the best they can.[3] The colloquial term used is 'working above the line'. The premise as it relates to resilience is that while we cannot avoid life's difficulties we can change the way we respond, learn from and build potential from these.

The material is provided in a practical and easy-to-read format that allows you to readily apply the principles and ideas to daily life at work. All activities and exercises are tried and proven and can be applied in most workplaces. Should you be interested in exploring any of the concepts in more detail, suggestions on further reading are provided at the back of the book.

Emphasis is on behaviours, approaches and thinking that you can use everyday in a variety of situations. While the focus is on building bounce back at work, the concepts are applicable to all parts of your life, including parenting. You will discover that as you start to build your resilience you cannot attain it without investment in your personal circumstances. Both are intertwined. We cannot just build resilience in specific parts of our daily lives; it requires a permanent shift in how we approach everything we do.

You may decide to focus on just one or two areas of resilience. If so reviewing the relevant chapters will give you an overview of what to do. At the end of each chapter a quick summary of its contents is also listed. You can use this to point you in the direction of ideas you may like to explore further.

Developing resilience is a personal journey. To gain maximum benefit from your reading it is best to work through each chapter slowly, completing the Bounce-Back individual exercises over an extended period. Keep your changes to small actions that you can do straight away. You will find this will make it easier to embed your new behaviours into daily activities.

Resilience is complex and, as with any personal growth, it will always be a work in progress, with scope to develop further. Small simultaneous shifts in a number of aspects of your behaviour can make a big difference.

There is a lot of material in this book, and you will need to choose what aspect to work on. Trying too much at once will not be sustainable. Everybody is different, so it is important to identify what works best for you and your circumstances and culture. We know too, that in order to deal with the broad variety of stressors we experience we need a tool-kit of strategies. No single approach will help in every situation. Use this book to expand the coping responses you have at hand when you need them.

In some cases you may be already familiar with the ideas. When this happens try not to fall into the trap of saying 'I already know that' or 'That's common sense'; instead, reflect on how well or often you are doing this and how you could do better. Many of the concepts may be simple but are not necessary easy to implement. 'Simple' rarely equates with 'easy' when we are attempting to change our behaviour. Just think when you last tried to give up chocolate or other vices. Changing routines and idiosyncrasies takes considerable time and effort, especially if you have a lifetime of habit to change. If you struggle in making personal changes, some tips on doing this are provided in Chapter 10.

Finally, while the book is aimed at assisting you the reader, you may also choose to promote these ideas with your colleagues. Regardless of your job, you can contribute to improving the work climate. You do not need to be a team leader to foster change as the small size of most teams allows each person to make a difference. Do you prefer to work in a supportive environment with a resilient team? Most people do, and you can help create this.

Just by modelling resilience you can help foster rebound ability in your whole team. If you do happen to be in a leadership position this is particularly beneficial as we know that the actions of leaders have a big impact on the work environment. A positive, open and adaptable leader fosters these attributes in others, while one who is negative, controlling or bad-tempered creates risk aversion and demotivation. Note, too, that what you do has far more influence on others than what you say. In a similar way to parenting it's a case of 'Do as I do, not do as I say!'

Chapter 1: Tips for understanding resilience

- You can learn to be more resilient despite your personal characteristics.
- Identify where you need to invest more energy — mental toughness, emotional balance, physical endurance, or life purpose.
- Work through the book and its activities slowly, applying ideas as you go.
- Make small shifts simultaneously in a number of aspects of your life. This makes a big difference overall.
- Role model resilience and foster it in others.

Reframing problems: Developing the right mindset

Men are not prisoners of fate, but only prisoners of their own minds.

Franklin D. Roosevelt

Mental toughness demands having the right mindset to address the daily difficulties of life. How you contemplate and think about any event dictates how you tackle it. If you are facing a challenge at work — for example, giving a presentation — negative thoughts such as 'I'm going to make a fool of myself' will increase your anxiety and impact on your performance. More importantly your overall thinking patterns influence not only how well you respond to life but also your health and wellbeing.

As our thought patterns are mostly learned in childhood they become so integral to our identity that our beliefs about how the world operates are often unconscious. The same applies to workplaces where beliefs can be so entrenched they become part of the organisation's culture, and described as 'the way we do things around here'.

Resilient thinking involves recognising unhelpful ways of thinking, as well as having perspective, and a deeper and broader understanding of events. It means being adaptable and solution-focused when problems and obstacles arise, and having a sense of optimism and hope.

As with any skill, we can learn to change our mindset with practice and effort. This chapter will heighten awareness of your thinking patterns and those of your work colleagues. It offers examples of common unhelpful thinking patterns and offers ideas on resilient ways to interpret and tackle daily events. As our thought processes are very individualistic, you will need to select the areas where you see most scope for personal improvement.

Put things in perspective

How's your wife? Compared to what?

Old Vaudeville joke

On any busy day, with multiple demands and deadlines to meet, it is easy to lose perspective about what is important and what is not. Under pressure it is not unusual to overreact to a minor event such as missing a phone call or a computer malfunction. Be honest — when was the last time you overreacted to a minor incident at home or work?

Unfortunately, when the pressure is constant these reactions can start to become typical rather than occasional. A key strategy for mental toughness at these times is putting things in perspective.

A simple way to gain perspective in any situation is to rate the event you are experiencing on a crisis line from 1–10. A rating of 1–2 would be a relatively minor event and a rating of five something fairly serious. Only events that are really traumatic such as death, divorce and disaster should rate at 9–10.

Crisis line

1	5	10
Small setback		Major crisis

When thinking about work events in this way, an equipment breakdown could be rated around 1 and the death of a colleague, 10.

Reflect back on a typical busy week at work and consider how consistent your responses have been with the actual importance of the events encountered. Chances are you moved to a rating of 9 when an appliance jammed or a supplier let you down with an urgent order.

In reality, most things that happen to us on a day-to-day basis are only around the 2 mark in overall life importance. Yet when we are stuck in a traffic jam on the way to an appointment or late with a report, our reaction can easily become a 7, a rating totally inconsistent with the importance of the event.

The difficulty is that our hectic pace of life means we are already operating at a 5–6 level. From this baseline it's easy to overreact to any setback and move to a crisis response of 8 or 9. When you reflect on the last time you overreacted, you may find it was just an insignificant incident that tipped you over as you were already at saturation point.

Crisis responses are unfortunately becoming part of daily life. Consider for a moment all of the new rages that have entered the common vernacular. We have road rage, phone rage, computer rage, car park rage, queue rage and even shopping trolley rage. What others have you heard of?

At work, regular overreaction to unexpected setbacks can create a climate of crisis management. If you have worked in a situation like this you will know this is not only draining, but can ultimately be demoralising as you start to feel you lack any control in your role. When energy is constantly focused on resolving the problem symptoms rather than addressing its sources, people can frequently get into mild panic over events that may not be important in the overall scheme of things.

Do you regularly lose perspective with particular incidents at work? If so ask yourself:

- How do I usually react?
- What impact is this reaction having?
- What can I say to myself to put these things in perspective?

Avoid the crisis response

> *One of the symptoms of an approaching nervous breakdown*
> *is the belief that one's work is terribly important.*
>
> Bertrand Russell

By reminding yourself to put things in perspective you can reinforce the overall importance of the event and adjust your reaction accordingly. Preventing the crisis response means calming down and asking yourself:

- How important is this in the bigger scheme of things?
- What is the worst thing that could happen here?
- What sort of energy and reaction does this event really warrant?

If you are in regular crisis mode an additional question may be: 'What steps can we take to prevent this happening next time?'

Aligning our reaction to the importance of the event can stop the crisis response and reduce the personal impact of the event. When small irritating episodes are frequently tipping us over the edge, perspective-taking may be one key to maintaining some equilibrium.

> ### BOUNCE-BACK ACTIVITY
>
> ## Gaining perspective
>
> Build into your work routines the opportunity to reflect on what went well and why. When you are stressed and busy it is easy to focus more on what's not working and how difficult things are. This can create a cycle of negativity.
>
> By regularly reflecting on what has gone well and the reasons behind this you can better appreciate your strengths and the positive aspects of your work. Identifying what is working also provides an opportunity to focus on doing more of this. It is always easier to leverage from what is working than experiment with other approaches.
>
> Perspectives such as 'That was an awful day, I'm glad it's over' can become 'I got through a huge workload by just putting my head down'.

Lighten up

> *If I were given the opportunity to present a gift to the next generation, it would be the ability for each individual to learn to laugh at himself.*
>
> Charles Schultz

Another twist on changing perspective is to lighten up and see the funny side of a situation. Standing back and seeing how ridiculous you must look arguing over a petty issue transports you out of the emotional heat of the moment.

Black humour is a common way of dealing with difficult situations and many professions with gruelling tasks such as emergency workers use this in various ways. If it's a colleague or your boss who is overacting and causing you distress, use mental imagery. Visualising your manager dressed as a toddler and throwing a teddy can defuse any intimidation quickly. The variations on the scenarios are only limited by your imagination!

Humour not only makes us feel better, it enhances our productivity and decision-making. When we are feeling light-hearted we tend to be more emotionally open, energised and more helpful and generous to others. Chapter 7 explores this further.

Let the small things go

Don't sweat the small stuff … But it's all small stuff!

Anonymous

Are your everyday stressors small frustrations that accumulate into overload? When you explode is it a case of the straw that breaks the camel's back?

We know that we need to let go of some of the small stuff but it's not that easy. A good illustration of this is the challenge of parenting teenagers. In an average week teenagers can provide plenty of angst, ranging from messy rooms and sloppy dress to taking drugs and staying out all night. Addressing everything you take exception to is not only exhausting and unfulfilling but produces push-back that just exacerbates the situation.

In these situations we need to choose our battles in order to win the war. Ask yourself 'What are the frustrations I can live with and what are those I'll stand fast on?' For teenagers, if their room is often a mess, take a photo of it when it's tidy and place it prominently on the door, keeping it closed. If it's drug taking then that's a different story. Letting the small things go will leave you with more energy and resolve for the important battles.

Apply the same principle at work. Your boss may have an irritating habit of delegating urgent tasks at the last minute. If you have negotiated without success, then expecting it and working around it may be easier than getting upset every time it happens. A colleague may constantly make snide remarks. If picking them up on this has made no difference, then smiling at them and considering it their problem not yours may be better than becoming resentful, angry or anxious. This is an example of a strategy that is simple but not easy. Allowing yourself to let go and change your usual response may be challenging — especially if you are convinced you are right.

Manage perfectionism

> *Ring the bells that still can ring*
> *Forget your perfect offering.*
> *There is a crack in everything,*
> *That's how the light gets in.*
>
> Leonard Cohen

Letting go of the small things is a particular challenge if you are a perfectionist. Very high personal standards and expectations not only create additional stress but make it even more difficult to adjust behaviour.

One practical way of tackling perfectionism is to gradually decrease the effort you put into less critical tasks and activities and watch and see if this is noticed. Chances are your managers and colleagues will be totally unaware that you have only proof-read once instead of twice, or that your desk or workstation is not as tidy and organised as it usually is. Confirmation that nobody has noticed can give you confidence to let other small things go. If the thought of this is too frightening you can start by practising at home. Clean and organise less and let go of your standards a little. It will then be easier to translate this confidence in letting go to work activities.

If you are holding back on work until you are 110% happy with its quality, another idea is to send documents out clearly marked as a draft. This will ensure you advance the work in some way rather than procrastinating over whether it's good enough to distribute.

Of greater difficulty is working on the underlying beliefs that drive your perfectionism. These can stem from deep-seated thoughts of not being good enough or needing to please others. Recognising this can be a positive first step, although over-analysing may not be that useful. Simply acting differently and noting the benefits is a practical way of starting to change.

Many people excuse perfectionism at work by claiming it is professionalism. Differentiating between the two is useful. Managing perfectionism does not mean dropping critical standards. It becomes a problem when your personal expectations become unmanageable, self-imposed demands that create more pressure than is needed. It is not permission for work sloppiness or low standards, rather it means spending less time on tasks that do not need the level of input you are providing. What are the acceptable standards of professionalism in your work and how do these compare with your own? With the busyness of workplaces these days, trying to achieve a benchmark of 110% perfect on everything can be a recipe for burnout. If you are a manager expecting this of others you may be setting yourself up for failure.

Focus your energy
Concentrate on the tasks that matter
A loss of perspective and adopting a crisis response also has implications for how we manage our time at work. On a daily basis we often need to distinguish what is urgent from what is important when setting our priorities. This distinction is called the Eisenhower Principle.[1] An expansion of this principle is the Ti-Mandi Window (time and I), a tool developed by UK management consultant John Nicholls (2001) and illustrated in Figure 2.[2]

The underlying philosophy of the Ti-Mandi tool is to prioritise work by importance rather than urgency. One of its aims is to avoid the crisis response of urgent tasks getting most of the attention regardless of their importance.

Typically we spent up to 80% of our work time in the 'trivial hot potato' (urgent, unimportant) category when we should be

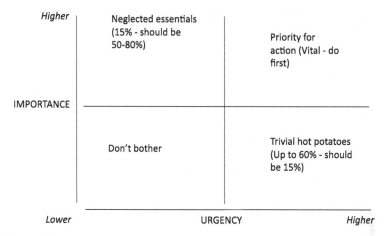

Figure 2
Ti-Mandi window adapted from Nichols (2001).

spending around 15%. In turn, while our activity on 'neglected essentials' should typically be 50–80%, it is more often around 15%. These non-urgent important tasks are generally those with a long-term or strategic focus that we put off until they finally become urgent. Without attending to work in this quadrant we remain fixed in the reactive mode. Ironically too, the busier we are the less time we seem to spend on these jobs and the more we feel we are not in control and doing our job properly.

One useful idea is to break down the non-urgent important tasks into smaller tasks and build completion of these into daily routines. Try creating non-negotiable space in your diary, or incorporate the work into team structures such as meetings and reporting. This will not only highlight the work but also reinforce its priority.

A very simple and practical way to stay on track is to keep two checklists that you update daily:

1. Things I need to do today.

2. Things I need to remember today.

BOUNCE-BACK ACTIVITY

Applying Ti-Mandi

■ Review whether you have the right balance between urgent and important tasks in your working week.

■ What for you are the 'neglected essentials' and how can you structure your work to do more of these?

■ What can be dropped from the 'trivial hot potatoes' quadrant, or completed more efficiently?

Guard against procrastination

When the going gets tough, the tough get going.

Billy Ocean

Another potential obstacle to progressing the longer-term, more important aspects of our work is procrastination. Are you a procrastinator? Do you put off the more difficult or challenging activities? Does worry about the outcome or what people may think prevent you even starting? Do others see you as indecisive?

Often we procrastinate because the sheer size of the task seems overwhelming. If this is the case for you, chunk it down into more manageable steps and just start the easiest task. Before you know it you will be halfway through something that seemed insurmountable. If you are in a state of indecision, decide to decide, and once you have chosen a path use your energy to make that work rather than wasting time agonising over what to do. The benefit of hindsight means we can sometimes regret decisions we made, yet in reality most decisions are the best ones for that point in time. We never know what is around the corner. Energy spent on procrastinating is much better spent on moving forward.

At other times we may procrastinate because of an underlying, often unrecognised, fear. Typically it is fear of rejection, fear of failure, fear of looking incompetent, or even fear of success itself. In these situations it is useful to name the fear and separate the real fears from the ones you have fabricated in your mind. Perhaps you are delaying making a follow-up phone call to an important client. An underlying fear of rejection could be the source of procrastination. Delaying the call will not change the outcome and may have the negative consequences of holding up progress in other aspects of your work. Also, any rejection is not likely to be personal, rather a commercial decision based on a better offer by a competitor. Conquering fears builds personal confidence as many fears prove unfounded once action is taken.

Finally, when addressing procrastination it helps to contemplate the worse case scenario and assess the probability of this happening. Ask yourself:

- What is the worst thing that could happen here?
- How likely is it that this will happen?
- Can I live with this happening?

As an example, if you are procrastinating about asking for a pay rise or flexible hours what is the worst thing that could happen? It's probably a resounding 'no' and a temporary dent to your self-esteem. In the meantime the chance of a 'yes' is lost in your procrastination.

Some of us have personalities that are more pessimistic and risk-averse. We expect the worst to happen. If this is you, you will need to work extra hard to overcome concerns by gradually taking small manageable risks until your confidence increases and procrastination lessens.

BOUNCE-BACK ACTIVITY

Pro-activity

Consider the following questions in relation to a project, task or idea that you have been procrastinating about:

▪ What is something easy you can do to just lead into it and get started?

▪ Is there something you can integrate into another task or project you are already doing?

▪ How can you publicly commit yourself to doing something? — Is there somebody you can tell? Is there an agenda item you can add to? Is there a promise you can make? Is there somebody you can get to help you out? Just getting started in any form immediately builds some momentum.

Visualise success

I dream my painting and then I paint my dream.

Vincent van Gough

Another way of building your confidence to take on challenging tasks you may be procrastinating about is to use the 'storyboard technique'. This technique is especially powerful as it combines mental rehearsal with the 'chunking down' approach described above.

Mental rehearsal involves using mental imagery to practise or rehearse something in your mind beforehand in order to make the actual event occur more easily. It is commonly used in fields as diverse as sport, business and therapy to enhance performance and build personal confidence.[3]

Storyboarding entails rehearsing positive outcomes by visualising in turn each of the steps needed to achieve your goal. To do this, first relax your body and mind and then visualise yourself successfully executing each step, then build this until the sequence can be seen as a full story. With each step, visualise yourself as competent, successful, and satisfied with its completion.

Focus on where you can make a difference

> *Lord, grant me the strength to change the things I can change;*
> *the serenity to accept the things I cannot change, and the wisdom*
> *to know the difference.*
>
> Prayer of Alcoholics Anonymous

At work, as in life, lots of things happen that are outside our control and influence. These can all be a source of worry. Take an organisational change or restructure, for example. Chances are we may have had limited input into this happening and may not be happy about its implications. It may mean a change in our role, working with different people or even decreased status, all of which may cause us concern.

If you concentrate on these concerns and the problems they are causing you, your focus becomes increasingly negative. You can start to blame others, become angry or resentful and ultimately find yourself in a victim trap, as illustrated in Figure 3.

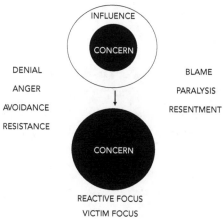

Figure 3
The victim trap.

Typically at work we blame management, even in times when we know there are other forces at work such as market changes. In these circumstances we see ourselves as passive recipients of circumstances outside of our control and resentment and negativity builds. In an unhappy workforce this can quickly take hold, resulting in low morale and discontent. Sometimes this can become so bad whole teams develop a state of paralysis while waiting for changes to happen that are outside of their influence.

Focusing your energy on problems and concerns leaves less space for problem-solving and improving your situation. The more negative you become the less motivation you will have. By contrast, focusing on the areas you can influence creates positive energy that can increase your impact. To shift to a sense of increased control you need to accept what you cannot change and learn to live with it even if you would rather not.

A simple strategy is placing your concerns into three imaginary buckets:

- one for the concerns you can influence
- one for the concerns you have no influence over
- one for the concerns where you are uncertain about your influence. Note though that you can only place these concerns temporarily in this bucket as they will need to eventually go into one of the other two!

What you then need to do is put all your energy into emptying the bucket with concerns you can influence, even though the reality is that this will be frequently topped up.

Creating collective focus on resolving problems in a team is especially advantageous. How can you work with colleagues to prevent, eliminate, reduce or simply change the interpretation of an issue you all face?

> **BOUNCE-BACK ACTIVITY**
>
> ## Focus on where you make a difference
>
> Consider a situation at work where there are events that are happening that are mostly out of your control and complete the following steps:
>
> ▌ List all the concerns you have about this situation.
>
> ▌ Work through the list and identify those areas where you have influence and can make a difference and those which you simply have to accept.
>
> ▌ For those areas where you can make a difference, develop an action plan to address these.

Assess your options

Remember, in any unsatisfactory circumstance where you cannot change the source of your angst, there are only three choices open to you:

- You can leave (although this is not always an option given financial or other commitments).

- You can put up with the situation and suffer the personal consequences such as resentment or anger, or

- You can accept the new reality or modify how you interpret and respond to the situation.

Which option you decide on will usually depend on how important the issue is and its potential impact on you. Putting up and shutting up may be more costly than leaving if you end up distressed and unhappy. For example, if you are in conflict with a colleague and have tried unsuccessfully to address this with the person and your manager, you will need to assess your personal fall-out. If your health is being affected, getting out is the best option. If you have no exit opportunities, reframing how you view and respond to the situation is the only positive path open. Often for things to change, you will need to change, even in situations when you are convinced you are right. Staying on the 'I'm right' tack can be a risk as a need to always be right can make you appear self-righteous.

Persist

> *Fall down seven times, get up eight.*
>
> Japanese proverb

Resilience means persisting despite obstacles. As humans we seem to be hard-wired to just try harder when actions aren't working for us. Often this just creates more push-back. While perseverance is admirable, a change of approach may be much healthier. Often, doing something completely different will work much better for you than continuing to act in the same manner. A change in tack may provide just the outcome you hope for. In essence, if it works, do more of it; if it doesn't, try another approach.

As an example, if your boss is discounting your ideas, you can become more and more assertive about them and risk putting him or her offside through challenging too often. A change in tack could be to influence your manager indirectly through other people. Another manager, a customer, or a colleague may get your ideas considered and achieve the outcome you want without an adverse impact on your relationship with your boss.

Challenge negativity

One of the most difficult aspects of being on a team can be working with negative or cynical colleagues. Just one doomsayer in a team can be emotionally draining and detract from constructive output. Like the dementers in the Harry Potter series, they can suck the energy from you. This is especially challenging in times of change or difficulty when teams are already over-whelmed.

If people are entrenched in cynicism the first step is to recognise that this is not necessarily about the current situation. It is more likely to be an accumulation of past experiences or a cynical disposition. The task is not to change their viewpoint, as this may be beyond rescue, but to ensure you do not foster or take on their negativity.

Agreeing in principle and offering a different perspective can be a useful way to respond to negativity in a positive but non-challenging way. Asking for their ideas may also assist in engaging people with a pessimistic outlook.

Here are some examples that may assist you in determining a response:

Comment: 'We'll never get that done we're already overworked.'

Response: 'Yes we're certainly busy, but amazingly we all seem to pull together and do what we need to do every day.'

Comment: 'That will never work.'

Response: 'You might be right but we need to at least give it a try to see if it will. It could make life easier for us.'

Comment: 'There are better ways than that to do it.'

Response: 'That's true, there would have to be. What do you suggest we try?'

Be sure to adopt a soft and positive tone of voice, as well as open body posture. Non-verbal communication is very powerful, and how you express yourself has more impact than what you say in most situations.

Responses like this are especially valuable in closing down gossip. In reality, the simplest way to stop gossip is to give it no airtime. Gossipers can perceive your listening as agreeing with them, so it is important to retort in some way. Here is an example of how you might respond:

Reframing negativity

Write your response to some of the typical negative workplace comments below.

'We've never done it that way before.'

'Why mess with what has worked well for the last ten years?.'

'That's against what we believe in.'

'We're stressed enough as it is.'

'They've got it wrong.'

'It looks good in theory, but it won't work in practice.'

'We tried something like that before and it didn't work.'

'I'm fed up of all these changes.'

What typical comments do you get and how might you provide a different perspective?

Comment: 'Did you hear about George's fallout with his manager?'

Response: 'That's George's business and we should keep out of it don't you think?'

Comment: 'We're all finding Mary difficult to work with — what about you?'

Response: 'It's fine as far as I'm concerned. Have you thought about talking directly with her about your concerns? She probably isn't even aware of them.'

Identify negative comments you regularly hear in your team and prepare your response. Practise it out loud a couple of times before trying it out. Talking out loud will not only help you improve your confidence in delivery but will also allow you to practise getting the right tone and level in your voice. It sounds silly but it works.

Remember though that negativity is not always bad. Criticism and challenge foster creativity and improve management of risk at work. While challenging continuously negative colleagues is important for our sanity, closing down routine critique will work against successful team outcomes.

Chapter 2: Tips for developing the right mindset

▮ Maintain perspective and avoid the crisis response.

▮ Lighten up and laugh at yourself.

▮ Spend your energy on the things that matter. Let the little things go.

▮ Guard against procrastination.

▮ Visualise success using the storyboard technique.

▮ Manage perfectionism without confusing it with professionalism.

▮ Focus your energy within your sphere of influence and accept events you have no influence over.

▮ Recognise you have only three options when the source of your discontent cannot be changed.

▮ Persist by changing tack rather than pushing harder in the same direction.

▮ Reframe negativity in yourself and others.

Embracing life:
More on mental toughness

The challenge of change

> *The times they are a-changing.*
>
> Bob Dylan

The phrase 'change is a constant' is hackneyed but true. None of us could ever have anticipated just how dramatically things have changed in our lifetime — politically, socially, economically and environmentally. The economic impact of the Global Financial Crisis and the speed of global warming, for example, were largely unpredicted and have fundamentally impacted on all aspects of our lives.

At work there have also been transformational changes. We have moved from a 9-to-5 day in a fixed place of work with a majority of male employees to the virtual diverse teams and 'hot desk' workspaces of today. Many occupations today did not exist 10 or even 5 years ago, and our children will have careers in jobs still not invented.

Typically our responses in times of rapid change and uncertainty are to seek comfort in routine and what we can control. This can narrow our focus as we try to keep things in order and arranged in the way they have always been. In reality, the more different or adverse the event is the more our familiar ways of thinking may be less effective in dealing with it. In fact, it is often the challenging events that need more flexibility in response. They also provide an opportunity to explore how we think and how helpful this thinking is.

Mental resilience in our complex and changing times requires a different approach — one of embracing rather than trying to control events. Life is unpredictable and complex and it is this that creates its richness. Pain and sadness are just as much a part of life as joy and happiness, and living through the tough times allows us to appreciate this. Experiencing anxiety and disappointment and converting this into positive action is the important skill. This involves a focus on solutions and a combination of optimism and hope.

Be solution focused

Problem talk creates problems. Solution talk creates solutions.

Steve de Shazer

Focusing on possibility rather than negativity is a key aspect of resilience. One of the most powerful ways you can model this in the workplace is through the language you use, especially when discussing problems or challenges.

Using solution-focused questioning is one very useful way of concentrating discussion on what is possible rather than what is not working. These questions are open-ended 'W' questions (what, when, where, who) that are framed towards the solution rather than the problem.[1]

Some examples ...

• What would it look like if this was working for us?

- How would it look if we achieved our goal?
- What tells us that we can do this?
- How can we use our strengths to resolve this?
- What would others notice if we achieved this?
- How will we know things are getting better?
- How do we want it to be different?
- When things are different what would we be doing that we are not doing right now? What small change could we make to progress this?

Note that the use of 'Why' should be avoided in these situations as it requires a justification in answering and can convey a negative tone. Use 'How come?' instead with an inflection that indicates curiosity in the response.

Placing attention on what you and your team desires rather than what is wrong effectively generates energy more quickly towards potential solutions. Ideas generated can then be translated into next actions. In a way it is starting with the end in mind.

The increasingly popular application of Appreciative Enquiry in organisations supports this strategy with its underlying premise that organisations move in the direction in which they enquire.[2]

Leverage what exists

You cannot teach anybody anything. You can only help them to discover it themselves.

Galileo Galilei

When we make attempts to change, either on our own or as a team, it is often easier to base our future actions on things that have already worked rather than learning or experimenting with completely new approaches. More often than not we have the resources we need, we just need to both recognise and capitalise on this. The philosophy is to build on what works rather than what doesn't.

An excellent and easy-to-use tool for recognising and leveraging our capabilities is 'scaling'. This simply involves asking yourself the following questions:

1. On a scale from 1 to 10, what number describes the progress you want to achieve?

2. Where would you say you are at the moment?

3. What is different now, compared to when you would have rated yourself as one rating lower?

4. What actions or strategies helped you move from a lower rating to where you are now?

5. How might you use these techniques to move up a rating?

As an example, imagine you want to procrastinate less, and you rate your current level of procrastination as 4 and your desired rating as 8. Start by imagining what it would look like if it was rated as an 8. Then identify what you currently do to rate it as 4 (rather than a lower score of 3). Finally determine potential actions to move from this rating of 4 to 5.

Posing some of the following questions may help generate tangible behaviours to improve ratings:

• How will you notice you have moved a step higher on the scale?

• How will people around you notice?

• What would you be doing that you are not yet doing?

• When you arrive at work tomorrow what would be the first small sign of progress?

Be flexible

Adaptability and flexibility are key components of resilience. Both characteristics are core aspects of our personality, which means that some of us will need to work harder than others to achieve this.

Avoid black and white thinking

It is not uncommon for people to think in terms of opposites. Things are either 'good or bad' or 'right or wrong'. At work we commonly call people like this 'black and white'. We see them as inflexible, with fixed views on life, work and other people. Convincing them to do something they do not believe in, or to work with somebody they have a poor opinion of, can be very challenging.

Consider whether you are guilty of fixed thinking and 'all or nothing' thoughts. Do you decide you are no good at something and quit quickly, or perhaps not even try in the first place as you have pre-determined its failure? Have you ever retorted with 'That's the way I am, there's nothing I can do about it'? Do you quickly write off or dismiss people?

While fixed thinking may be useful when we have to make rapid decisions, rarely are events simplistic enough to be black or white. The world we work in demands constantly working and adapting within the 'shades of grey'.

If anybody has accused you of thinking in this way you may need to listen more to others' opinions and be open to exploring issues before making a judgment. In workplaces all of us have to adapt our thinking and behaviours, and stating that we don't have capacity to do this is avoiding personal responsibility. We simply can't take the 'That's the way I am stance'. Being inflexible can be exhausting, both in terms of arguing and maintaining a stance, as well as difficult for those who have to work with you.

If fixed thinking is characteristic of several of your colleagues, you may find team decision-making is difficult, with each person arguing for their viewpoint. A useful approach when there are strong opposing views is to use a problem-solving model such as Edward De Bono's *Six Thinking Hats*,[3] or the Isakawa diagram[4]. These tools are very effective in shifting attention to all the factors and information to be considered in a problem, rather than arguing a particular stance. There are a wide variety of instruments freely available on the internet to choose from. Introducing these to your team may help in mapping issues and listing options before you progress to agreeing on actions.

With practice in using problem-solving tools and frameworks, teams can become quite adept at collaborative problem-solving, and more open to different possibilities.

Turn adversity into opportunity

My advice is to find fuel in failure. Sometimes failure gets us closer to where we want to be.

Michael Jordan

British psychologist Richard Wiseman spent 10 years investigating what makes people believe they are lucky. After hundreds of studies and interviews with lucky and unlucky people he found that luck is not a gift but a state of mind — a particular way of thinking and behaving. In essence, he scientifically proved the traditional wisdom 'You make your own luck'. Five principles of luck were identified which, not surprisingly, all relate to how you view life and respond to it.

One of the key principles Wiseman discovered was that lucky people had not lived a charmed life.[5] In fact, many of those who considered themselves lucky had endured considerable hardship and obstacles. What they had learned to do was to find the opportunity in the adversity, the silver lining in the cloud as it were.

Often major turning points occur in our lives through challenging and unexpected events. A job loss, accident or the death of a close friend or relative can frequently be the event that creates a new direction. For example, many people who have reinvented their career after being retrenched would not have done this without circumstances precipitating or even forcing it.

Mental resilience involves reframing your view of setbacks you experience while simultaneously searching for any new opportunity it presents. Lucky people are adept at discovering ways to turn the inevitable bad luck we all experience into good fortune.

Lucky people are also able to maintain optimism during the setback, the next topic in this chapter. A verse of the famous poem 'If', featured above the doorway to centre-court Wimbledon, expresses this succinctly:

> *If you can dream — and not make dreams your master;*
> *If you can think — and not make thoughts your aim;*
> *If you can meet with Triumph and Disaster*
> *And treat those two impostors just the same.*
>
> Rudyard Kipling

BOUNCE-BACK ACTIVITY

Opportunity in adversity

Reflect on a recent negative experience and search for the silver lining in the event.

▮ Is there an opportunity?

▮ Is there a learning?

▮ Is there capacity for personal growth?

Develop optimism

> *The difficult is done immediately, the impossible takes just a*
> *little longer.*
>
> Unofficial motto of the US Marine Corps

Success at work is not just dependent on talent and drive, but also on our attitude to success and failure — that is, our level of optimism. The more your job involves persistence, initiative and dealing with frustration and rejection the more optimism you need.

Research has linked optimism to positive mood, good morale, perseverance, wellbeing and even effective problem-solving. According to a study by Harvard Medical School, optimistic people also live 19% percent longer. They also have better physical health and are less susceptible to depression. What's more, they are also fun to be around. It's a case of dying young as late as possible.

Psychologist Martin Seligman defines optimism as having three components: personalisation, permanence and pervasiveness.[6] The following scenario, summarised in the box on the opposite page, Optimistic Outlooks, explains what is meant by each of these concepts.

Jenny and Amelia both apply for a promotion. Both are talented and hardworking team members who have the same potential and opportunity for success. Jenny, however, is quite optimistic, while Amelia is pessimistic. Both end up missing out on the opportunity, but how they interpret the setback is quite different. Jenny, the optimist, does not *personalise* it. She understands that the competition was tough and she did all she could in the circumstances. Amelia, however, sees it as her fault; she personalises the failure. Jenny also sees this as a temporary setback. She has learned a lot from the selection process and is ready to try again. Her colleague Amelia, however, sees the event as more *permanent,* a loss of the only promotional opportunity she may get. Finally, the friends differ in how they are able to compartmentalise the event in their lives. Jenny remains buoyant with the other things going on around her while Amelia is generally down and the setback is *pervasive,* impacting on everything.

Note it is exactly the same situation for each of the colleagues, both of whom have the same potential. The difference is how they interpreted the event. If the event had been a positive one they would have also seen it differently, with Amelia attributing it to luck, rather than personal qualities, wondering how permanent it will be and not letting the success spill over to other parts of her life.

Optimistic Outlooks		
Perspective	Pessimistic outlook	Optimistic outlook
Personalisation	'It's my fault'	'It's not my fault'
Permanence	'This is the way it will always be now'	'This is just a temporary setback'
Pervasiveness	'My whole life is affected'	'I'm not going to let this affect anything else in my life'

Optimism can also create a spiral of increasing belief in our potential. Figure 4 below demonstrates the spiral of potential and setback that can develop out of scenarios such as that of Jenny and Amelia's job applications.

The message is that life is not the way it is supposed to be, it is the way it is. Your response to life's challenges determines your experience of life.

Even if you were not born with a 'sunny disposition' you can learn to adopt more optimistic ways of thinking. As parents

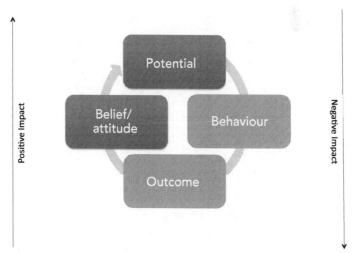

Figure 4
The potential spiral.

we should role-model optimism, and ensure that as our children grow and develop they gain as many opportunities as possible to experience success. The same principle applies to role-modelling at work, especially if we are in a leadership position, as optimism is infectious and needs to be led from the front.

Avoid blind optimism

> *The wise worm gets up late.*
>
> A twist on an old proverb

While optimism is generally preferable, there are always situations where a dose of pessimism is realism. Applying the Polyanna principle[7] in high-risk situations where there are high physical, emotional or financial challenges is simply blind optimism. The advice 'Don't worry be happy' fails to acknowledge that caution is also needed in life.

We need flexible optimism: the capacity to look on the bright side but also to be cautious when we need to. While optimists can embrace realism, pessimistic people find it more difficult to adopt a positive outlook.

Think optimistically

> *I have not failed. I've just found 10,000 ways that won't work.*
>
> Thomas Alva Edison

Increasing your optimism is simple but not easy as it involves recognising and changing your self-talk. Self-talk is the voice or tape in your head that provides a continuous commentary on life. It's the loudest voice we ever hear!

We know that on average 80% of our self-talk has some degree of negative content — it's the voice that says 'You're too fat to wear that', or 'You'll never get that promotion'. These negative thoughts produce negative feelings that in turn make us less able to perform in the way we would like to. Much of what we say to ourselves may be automatic, and we may not particularly notice our scripts except when situations require us to solve a new or difficult problem.

Read through the following typical examples of negative self-talk related to work. As you do, contemplate the feelings that would be associated with these thoughts and how that emotion would predict what you would do.

- 'These deadlines are getting more and more unrealistic.'
- 'What if they find out I haven't done a project exactly like this before?'
- 'I think it's a good idea but what if they don't?'
- 'I'm going to look a fool if they ask me a question I can't answer at my presentation.'

Now reflect on possible rewrites of these statements below and how these may change your subsequent behaviour.

- 'Just focus on one thing at a time and you'll get through it.'
- 'I'll do what I can and ask for assistance on the parts I do not understand.'
- 'It's a good idea; if it's rejected at least they will see I am taking the initiative on improving things around here.'
- 'I know more about this topic than the audience and that is why they've asked me to speak.'

Challenging and changing your self-talk when accompanied by confident posture will make you look calm and in control. To a large extent it's a case of fake it until you make it, as even the most polished performers will privately confess that they are nervous in some situations even though they appear confident. This appearance of being calm and in control is especially important in leadership positions as any sense of uncertainty or panic will filter down and increase anxiety within a team. An integral part of any manager's job is to buffer staff from major issues and instil confidence in their ability to manage difficult challenges.

Build hope

I have a dream that one day on the red hills of Georgia the sons of former slaves and the sons of former slave owners will be able to sit down together at the table of brotherhood.

Martin Luther King

Closely connected to optimism is holding hope. When times are tough at work this can sometimes be the only thing that keeps us going. It may be, for example, hope that the workload will ease off, hope the restructure will be finalised or hope that our job is secure.

As with optimism, hope can be self-generated and to build it you need to have:

1. the energy, belief and motivation to achieve your goal, and

2. multiple pathways to get there so that when one is blocked there are other avenues open.

Maintaining your personal belief and energy as well as having alternate pathways to your goals maintains hope. In practical terms it is creating both a mental and practical bridge to where you want to be. Not believing you can get there and stopping at the first obstacle is unhopeful thinking. As an example, if we are hoping for a promotion simply getting interview practice will not suffice. We also need to explore other opportunities available, enhance our skills and do anything that is going to better increase our chances of getting a more senior role. If we then miss out on the current position we still have other avenues to follow. Note that this does not mean that hope is the plan, rather that a solid plan builds hope.[8]

Specific advice on how to stay motivated towards the goals once you develop them is outlined in Chapter 10.

BOUNCE-BACK ACTIVITY

Noting self-talk

Catch your negative self-talk by writing the thoughts down then rewriting them in a positive way. Writing them down is especially useful as in black and white they appear far less plausible and subsequently less powerful.

Address negative thoughts

Do you have recurring negative thoughts that can sometimes overwhelm you and cause you anger, panic, worry or loss of confidence? If this is the case techniques beyond a re-write of your self-talk may be helpful.

Try the following two approaches and assess which one works best for you.

Argue with yourself

This involves three steps in disputing your self-talk:

1. Write down what you are saying to yourself — for example: 'I'm not good enough' or 'My manager doesn't believe I am up to the job'.

2. Ask yourself: 'Where is the evidence to support this?' or 'What could be another way of looking at this?' Argue with yourself that you are wrong.

3. Change your thoughts to those that better reflect the reality of the situation, as opposed to your perception of it.[9]

Defuse the thought

When thoughts are especially overwhelming you may find that any focus on them only makes you more anxious and less able to escape from them. You may also find that if your confidence is especially low in a situation, self-talk too incompatible with your real feelings may actually impair positivity.

In these situations defusion may help.[10] The aim of defusion is not to get rid of the thoughts, nor to change them to what you would like them to be. Instead the aim is simply to let them be there without fighting them, recognising them for what they really are — just words in your head.

The premise is that we take the stories we compile in our heads as truth, but really these thoughts are just words and nothing more. Try out one of these ideas to defuse your thoughts:

- Put them to the tune of 'Happy Birthday'.
- Say them in the voice of a cartoon character.
- Call them a story, such as the 'I'm not valued' or 'Nobody cares about me' story.
- Put the words on a screen and change the colour and style of the font.
- Say to yourself: 'I notice that I have a thought that I'm not valued/nobody cares about me.'

As you practise, notice how these actions can give you some distance from what you are thinking. This distancing in turn diminishes the power of the thought.

BOUNCE-BACK ACTIVITY

'What if?'

Are you worrying about a future event and only seeing the negative possibilities? For example, during an economic downturn you may worry: 'What if I lose my job?' or 'What if I'm given a new role I can't do?'

If there is an issue you are anxious about, write out five 'what if' statements with good potential outcomes. For example, for an organisational restructure you could write 'What if I get a chance to learn new skills?' or 'What if I get transferred closer to home?' While these thoughts will not change the outcomes, they will make you more energised and hopeful during the period of uncertainty. They may also provide a new direction or focus that you had not previously considered.

Chapter 3: Tips for mental toughness

▌ Focus on solutions not problems. Ask 'W' questions and work with the desired end in mind.

▌ Leverage and build on the resources you already have.

▌ Be flexible and adaptable in your thinking and interactions. Avoid black and white thinking.

▌ Accept that change is constant and embrace it rather than worry about it.

▌ Look for and capitalise on the opportunity in setbacks you encounter.

▌ Develop flexible optimism, employing pessimism in risky situations.

▌ Stay hopeful by believing in yourself and creating multiple pathways to your goal.

▌ Develop ways to dispute or defuse negative thoughts and thinking.

Investing in self-care: Getting the body right

I have the body of an eighteen-year-old. I keep it in the fridge.

Spike Milligan

Do you invest in your body what you expect to get out of it on a daily basis? Have you the physical stamina to get through the day?

To be physically resilient you do not necessarily need a high level of fitness or a rigid dietary regime, you just need to be physically equipped to do what you need to do. If you are reasonably healthy and working in a job that is not too physically demanding, small changes in routine may be all that's needed.

Ideas on how to build physical endurance are explored in this and the following chapter. Given we are inundated with tips for healthy living focus here is on strategies for the working day as opposed to general lifestyle.

Invest in self-care

The increasing pace of life has overwhelmed us with a sense of busyness. The standard greeting has become 'How are you going — busy?' We feel obliged to say we are flat out even when we are not.

When others are in a state of constant activity we can sometimes feel guilty if we are relaxed or unoccupied.

In our workplaces the stress of work demands can generate a range of health problems such as insomnia, headaches, anxiety, depression, skin disorders, heart disease and mood change. What's more, many of us can add problems in our personal life to the list of stressors that impact on our work performance.

Staying on top of the workload and balancing it with our home commitments requires constant investment in self-care. We need to know and manage our early warning signs and body rhythms, get enough sleep and ensure time out for relaxation. Looking after ourselves is a little like putting health as well as money in the bank for our retirement.

Recognise the signs of overload

When you are under pressure and doing more than usual, your body reacts with early warning signs. These may be changes in health, attitude, or behaviour that if left unrecognised may become more serious.

Knowing your warning signs enables you to take action earlier. Investment in your wellbeing at this stage will stop you progressing to longer-term ill health.

We each have different early warning signs that signal we are not coping. All arise out of our seven bodily systems, which include our emotional, cognitive, sympathetic, parasympathetic, muscular, endocrine and immune systems.

The box on the opposite page, Symptoms of Overload, summarises the typical early warning signs we may experience. Note which ones you have a tendency to experience. You may find that your symptoms are confined to one or two bodily systems. For example, you may be prone to become more emotional that usual, with mood swings and irritability, or you may find your immunity suffers and you continually get colds and flu that you cannot shake off.

Symptoms of Overload

Muscular system	Muscular aches and pains (such as back, neck and jaw) Nervous tics or gestures (such as foot tapping) Stuttering Tension headaches Grinding teeth
Emotional system	Mood swings Mild depression Anxiety or feeling less in control Irritability or frustration Inability to focus
Sympathetic nervous system	Migraine headaches Chest pain Hyperventilation High blood pressure/increased heart rate Dizziness or palpitations Increased perspiration
Parasympathetic nervous system	Stomach pain or cramping Changed eating habits (overeating, undereating) Nausea Constipation or diarrhoea Sexual difficulties Dry mouth or throat
Endocrine system	Skin rashes Thyroid difficulties Menstrual problems
Cognitive system	Negative thoughts Insomnia Poor concentration and memory Indecisiveness Racing thoughts
Immune system	Allergies Low-level infections Frequent bouts of colds or flu Hives

If you are susceptible to a particular health condition such as headaches, sleep disruption or anxiety, you will find that the onset or intensity of these will often increase during stressful periods.

The lesson here is to actively pay attention to the onset of any symptoms and respond by investing more in looking after yourself. If you don't, the physical and psychological changes may develop into longer-term, more serious health issues.

It is important to note though, that if you are experiencing changes in your health you should identify the underlying source. While you might assume stress is producing the symptoms, a proper medical diagnosis when you are experiencing problems is critical.

Avoid burnout

We use the term burnout to describe when people are feeling generally worn out with limited energy and motivation. Typical signs are feeling emotionally and physically exhausted with a sense of inadequacy and ineffectiveness. Sometimes cynicism also creeps in and we start to depersonalise our clients, patients or customers.

Interestingly, those most likely to suffer burnout are highly motivated professionals who are driven by ideal perspectives and a desire for high-quality outcomes. When the day-to-day realities of the job compromise these principles their work can lose its sense of meaning — a central aspect of resilience, as explored in Chapter 8.

Burnout is said to arise when the demands of our job exceed the resources we have available. The Jobs-Demands-Resources (JD-R) model developed by Professor Arnold Bakker and shown in Figure 5 demonstrates succinctly this interplay between resources and demands.[1]

Put simply, we need a balance between job demands and job resources in order to stay motivated and engaged rather than burnt out. While we need some demands to make our work challenging

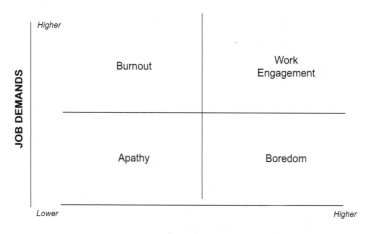

Figure 5
Job-Demands-Resources Model.

and interesting and to avoid boredom, too many of these without the means to manage them is stressful and overwhelming. On the other hand, when our resources meet the difficult demands we face the challenge becomes an event we can savour.

Examples of typical resources and demands we experience in our jobs are listed in the box on the following page, Workplace Resources and Demands. Which of these are relevant to you and how does your balance look like at the moment? It is worth noting that it is the perception of this balance that is important. What seems to be manageable to you, for example, may be seen as overload by a co-worker.

You may also find it useful to differentiate between the demands that you see as challenges and those you see as hindrances. Achieving the right balance involves maintaining the challenges with appropriate support in place, while simultaneously removing or better managing the hindrances. If the hindrance cannot be removed or minimised, reframing it positively, as outlined in Chapter 2 may be the only option open. As an example,

Workplace Resources and Demands

Examples of demands

Workplace level	Lack of job clarity
	Unclear responsibilities
	Role conflict
	Inadequate equipment
	Noisy work environment
	Shift work
	Budgets
	Work overload
	Poor leadership and management
	Poor work practices or systems
	Change
	Micro managemnet
Personal level	No involvement in decision-making
	Lack of autonomy
	Inadequate support
	Lack of empowerment
	Work conflict
	Inadequate or non-constructive feedback

Examples of resources

Workplace level	Team cohesion and support
	Adequate budget and resources
	Efficient work processes
	Joint team problem-solving
	Effective leadership and management
Personal level	Confidence
	Creativity
	Time and other self-management skills
	Energy
	Debriefing opportunity
	Influence
	Communication skills and channels
	Acknowledgment
	Collegial support
	Personal motivation
	Appreciation

extra responsibility you have been given could be seen as providing more personal influence or autonomy. A tight deadline can be reframed as getting the tasks out of the way more quickly.

While the JD-R model is presented here in relation to your work situation, it is impossible to separate your job and your personal life. Increased pressure or demands in any aspect of our lives has an immediate impact on our personal stress. Equally, resources from home such as the support of family and friends can assist us in staying on top of work pressures.

The most important aspect of this model as it relates to resilience is to recognise that the more pressure you are under, the more you need to invest in self-care at home and at work. Unfortunately, the reverse is often the reality. The more stress we experience the more likely we are to revert to bad habits and feel that we can't be bothered. We eat poorly, are too busy to socialise or relax, and feel too tired to exercise.

Increase personal resources

As described earlier it is important to take a holistic view of managing overload. The reality is that our lifestyle is defined to a greater extent by what we do outside of work than what we do during working hours.

In our private life there are a vast array of ways to manage pressure, and what works for you will be unique. We know that hobbies and creative pursuits are important in stress relief and that more passive activities, such as taking a bath, assist us to wind down.

The box on the following page, Personal Resources gives a very brief overview of the range of activities you could consider. Some of these involve active involvement, such as sport, while others like aromatherapy are more relaxing and passive. A combination of passive and active relaxation is ideal, as we need activities that relax the mind as well as the body. Weeks filled with active relaxation may not provide the wind-down time you need.

Personal resources	
Hobbies and creative pursuits	Massage
Sport	Shower/spa
Tai Chi	Yoga
Socialising/catching up with friends	Meditation
Playing with children	Aromatherapy
Spending time with pets	

Look after your physical wellbeing at work

Do you find it more difficult to focus on self-care at work than at home? Many people do. If this is the case, small shifts in your routines, such as eating regularly, pacing yourself and taking opportunities to move around can promote self-care on the job. Try the following tips for the working day.

Eat well

I never worry about diets. The only carrots that interest me are the number you get in a diamond.

Mae West

Eat properly and ensure you have lunch. Keep a stock of nutritious snacks such as nuts and dried fruit for emergencies when you can't get away from work for a break. That way when you need a lift to get you through you are less likely to reach for that chocolate bar or coffee.

Pace yourself

Slow down and everything you are chasing will come around and catch you.

John De Paola

There seems to be an increasing belief that faster is better because it saves time. Twitter, Facebook, SMS, email, abbreviated language, takeaway food, mini holidays, speed dating and adver-

> ## BOUNCE-BACK ACTIVITY
>
> ### Self-care at home
>
> Write a list of potential wind-down/relaxation activities and place it on the fridge or another prominent place at home. Make the actions specific and small; for example, take the dog for a walk, work on my painting, take a hot bath, ring my cousin, hit some golf balls. Be sure to include a combination of passive and active activities.
>
> Randomly choose an item from the list two to three times a week. In weeks where you are noticing early signs of overload, increase the number of these activities you do.
>
> You can also apply this principle at work to a lesser extent by listing a number of easier or enjoyable tasks that you can do when you feel tired or overwhelmed. This will give you a sense of continued productivity without overloading you further. Cleaning, clearing your email, sorting the stock or filing are all examples of routine tasks that may not need as much energy or focus. Interspersing these with enjoyable tasks such as networking or designing a brochure can help maintain your motivation.

tising grabs are just a few examples of how we have embraced this philosophy.

Speed has its costs though. The sheer pace of life means less time for reflection. Take emails as an example: the quantity we receive and the expectation of quick response times means we spend less time composing than we might when writing a letter. Reflecting on, and considering our response, can sometimes be a luxury, and regular fall-out occurs from hastily sent emails. Innovation also needs space for reflection and can be lost in our focus on quick responses.

A shortening attention span created by technology and fast living is also lowering our boredom threshold. The more stimulation we have the more we need it. It's similar to an addiction where we need instant response and gratification. We expect everything to entertain us and to have it now. We are only now accumulating evidence of the addictive power of smart phones, video games and other electronic devices. How easily are you able to ignore the message alert on your email or phone?

The downside of a fast life is no time to smell the roses and a sense that you always need to be quick to be efficient. Indirectly, this increases our level of tension and need for stimulation. Slowing down and pacing yourself is one way of counteracting this. Just by taking an extra one to two seconds to do things can mean the difference between feeling calm and controlled, or busy and tense. Not surprisingly, our actions do not appear slower to anybody else, and we end up being more efficient as we are more focused. It's a case of more haste less speed.

Pacing is especially important if you are a manager or a team leader as staff feel more assured if their manager looks in control rather than, as they say in Australia, 'Walking around like a chook with its head cut off'. It's a very simple shift that can have a big impact on our sense of being in control and the perceptions others have of how we are coping.

Take breaks

Taking mini breaks during the day can also reduce or prevent symptoms of tension. These breaks never need to take more than a few minutes and pay for themselves by making you more alert and productive. Studies have shown that problem-solving time can increase up to 500% if you work too long at mental tasks. Whenever we work on sustained tasks, we need to take strategic breaks by disengaging briefly and changing mental focus every 20–30 minutes. Without these planned pauses the brain unplugs anyway and we space out, doze off and lose concentration. 'Presenteeism' is the word used to describe this sense of when the body is there but the mind absent. Some managers describe it as 'when the lights are on but nobody's home'.

Another idea is to try to set up your day so that you shift between pleasant and more difficult tasks. After something tough try to schedule something you enjoy, that way the day does not seem so demanding. You should also ensure you take a meal break.

Move around

I am pushing sixty. That is enough exercise for me.

Mark Twain

If your work is fairly sedentary, capitalise on every opportunity to move around. Take the stairs or walk to a colleague's office. Light physical activity is one of the best ways to raise energy.

You can also take advantage of lunch breaks to do things that reduce tension, such as a brisk walk, a chat with friends, a relaxation exercise, or a bask in the sunshine. Get outside if you can and invite others to join you. Make it a routine to have a walk-and-talk meeting or some physical exercise. Fresh air can lift energy levels when you are inside all day. It also gives you a better sense of having a real break.

Office-bound teams keen on promoting physical activity use pre- and post-work time and lunch hours for shared activities such as walking, running, yoga, gym or sport. This has the advantage of both engaging peer pressure for motivation and creating a culture of physical exercise during the day. Making this interesting through having challenges or competitions can also increase participation and team cohesion. Catering to all levels of fitness is possible.

Create a relaxing space

If you are fortunate enough to have your own work area try to create a space that is personal and relaxing. Place personal effects around you and pay attention to posture ergonomics and light. All of these can impact on your wellbeing.

You could also use aromatherapy. Use lavender oil for calming and the uplifting citrus oils such as lemon and orange when you want to concentrate.

When you work in an open office area with constant interruptions, it may be necessary to schedule quiet time to complete tasks requiring concentration. If your desk is in a busy area find a quiet spot to sit. Let others know you are not to be disturbed. An 'open door policy' does not need to apply to the whole of the working day, and a routine 'do not disturb' time soon becomes known and accepted. Many people find they need this time out to complete work.

In busy work areas where you cannot control workflow, such as a shop, hospital or customer service counter, a relaxing area for breaks is important.

Pay attention to your energy levels

Paying attention to your energy levels and body rhythms during the day can help enhance your work effectiveness. Determine when you perform optimally and try to schedule difficult tasks at these times. If you are a morning person, for example, make the difficult meetings and tasks first thing in the day; if you are energised later in the day, use that time to work on tasks that need sustained concentration.

Aim for a state of calm energy. Characterised by low tension and high energy, this is the state when we feel alert, optimistic and energised.[2] It is quite different from the more commonly experienced tense energy (high tension and high energy), which can lead to burnout. In a tense energy mode we are driven almost by a sense of excitement and power, despite high levels of stress, and push ourselves further despite early warning signs. Many of us have worked with people who are driven. While most of us can sustain this for short periods of time, working like this over long periods is detrimental to our wellbeing, and often our relationships.

You can only achieve a calm energy state when you feel in control of what is happening and appreciate the need for pacing and relaxation.

Minimise negative coping strategies

It is easy to revert to poor habits when we are under pressure. We are more likely to reach for and enjoy that extra alcoholic drink, cigarette or coffee. While these responses may give us a lift in the short-term, the effects are, as we know, counter to good health and positive coping.

Take holidays

Increasingly, people complain that they cannot get away for holidays. Sometimes this is a fear of the work that will accumulate while they are away and the thought of the number of emails in the in-box. Other times it's a sense of being indispensable.

Holidays are critical times for rejuvenation and gaining perspective. It takes at least a couple of days for most people to wind down, so mini breaks are not ideal. If you are a leader in your organization, taking leave — in a similar way to taking breaks during the day — provides a role model for expectations and sets the scene for the unwritten organisational rules about taking time out.

Many organisations are now enforcing leave in recognition of its importance for staff wellbeing. At the end of the day though, it is our responsibility to ensure we take the holidays we need.

Early morning energisers

> *The amount of sleep required by the average person is five minutes more.*
>
> Wilson Mizener

If you are a night owl or struggle early in the morning, try some of the following tips to get up and going:

Expose yourself to bright light: Light naturally helps to wake us up. Our biorhythms for sleeping and waking are controlled by the hormone melatonin. Normally melatonin goes up when we fall asleep and down when we wake up. Light helps diminish the impact of the hormone on our body after a night's sleep and consequently alerts us. Exposure to natural light is preferable to artificial light as this light operates your biological clock and so provides a more accurate indicator of the time of day. Note that as a lot of light can keep melatonin levels down, working late in the evening on a computer can make it difficult to go to sleep.

Stretch: Light stretching loosens tight joints and muscles.

Shower: Showering or wetting your face is arousing.

Warm up: As your body temperature increases so does your level of alertness. Warming up your body can therefore help you feel more alert. This is best done through some sort of cardiovascular exercise.

Rehydrate: Drink a glass of water or herbal tea. Most people are dehydrated when they wake up, making them feel sluggish.

Have breakfast: A good breakfast is vital for replenishing our energy stores, which have depleted overnight. It has an instant and lasting effect. Avoid the 'I haven't got time' excuse for skipping this important meal.

Exercise outdoors: A burst of fresh air and natural light with exercise will instantly help you feel awake.

Create a work–home transition

Just as we need to create calm energy at work, we need to end the day by letting go of work issues, winding down slowly. This is easier said than done, and we can end up after a busy day feeling exhausted but unable to relax feeling tense or anxious. The cycle is exacerbated when we become too tense to sleep and then wake up tired for the start of another busy day. The 'to do' lists and forgotten tasks play on our minds and hinder relaxation.

One strategy is to try to create a work–home transition by ending your workday with less pressured tasks. Plan the next day if possible, or introduce a wind-down time when you get home before starting on other activities. You could have a shower, spend time talking with the children, take the dog for a walk, or just sit and have a drink. Having a regular routine will help better end your working day. If you have work to do at home, make it non-negotiable to relax and unwind first. Even more symbolic is using space for transition. Spending time showering in the bathroom or sitting in the bedroom before interacting with the family, for example, can help in moving from a work to a home mindset.

You can also use travel time to relax and make the transition. If you drive, play your favourite music or listen to an easy listening radio station. If you catch a train or bus, read a book or magazine that is unrelated to work. If you can walk, run or ride this is even better as the physical exercise will help you unwind, and you will then feel physically as well as mentally tired.

Choosing home leisure activities that balance the stressors of your job is also useful. If you spend a lot of time sitting and concentrating, for example, get involved in activities with aerobic exercise. If you work alone, socialise, and if you deal with conflict, choose peaceful pursuits. This balance will help counter the stressors of work.

Chapter 4: Tips for self-care

▮ Know the early warning signs of being overloaded and take action to rebalance the demands and resources in your work and home life.

▮ Actively invest in your self-care by eating well, exercising and taking time out.

▮ Pace yourself and slow down and smell the roses.

▮ Know and work with your body rhythms.

▮ Create a culture at work that promotes self-care. Take breaks, move around, be attentive to energy levels.

▮ Monitor and avoid burnout.

▮ Create a transition from work to home, allowing the stressors of work to be left behind.

Rejuvenating the body: More on physical endurance

To maintain our physical endurance we need to rejuvenate our body through good sleep and mental relaxation. Simple ideas on how to do this are outlined in this chapter. In the same way as we invest in our physical health through good exercise and nutrition we can invest daily in activities that promote our mental wellbeing.

Tips for better sleep

> *A good laugh and a long sleep are the best cures in the doctor's book.*
>
> Irish proverb

Changes in our quality of sleep are common symptoms of work overload. During stressful periods, frequent waking and general restlessness can all add to a drained feeling before you even get out of bed.

Exactly what happens during sleep is not fully understood, although we do know the body repairs and restores itself. Sleep is vital to keep your mind and body functioning properly. A good night's sleep can dramatically raise alertness, increase energy, enhance observational skills, boost motivation and measurably improve your performance.

On the flip side, sleep deprivation can have the same impact on our bodies as excessive alcohol, as any new parent will attest. Our performance can deteriorate with reduced focus, irritability and a general lack of energy and motivation. If this is prolonged our health can suffer. We may experience increased appetite, impaired immunity and even earlier onset of age-related illness.

The accumulated cost of missed sleep is called 'sleep debt'. As your sleep debt increases so does your body's desire to sleep. Most adults have too much sleep debt. This can be demonstrated by placing a person in a room to sleep without any day cues such as windows or clocks. They will sleep an extra 25 to 30 hours over the first two weeks in so called 'debt repayment'.

Ensure you have the amount of sleep you need. For the average adult this is 8 to 9 hours a night, although this depends on age, job demands and whether you are a 'morning' or 'evening' person.

Sleep patterns vary over our life span, with a common myth being we need less sleep as we get older. The quality of sleep does deteriorate with age due to higher incidences of disorders like sleep apnoea and menopause-related problems. This means older people often sleep less at night or have more disruptive sleep patterns, but as many nap during the afternoon the amount of sleep over the 24-hour period does not change.

How easy we find it to sleep or wake up is determined by our biological clock. Some scientists suggest that the time you are born affects these preferences. People born in Europe between April and September are more likely to be 'evening' people while those born between October and March are more likely to prefer mornings. One suggestion is that this is due to the day length during pregnancy.

If you are a shift worker you may find it hard to get the required amount of sleep with your body clock frequently disrupted. Sleep during the day can be difficult as light prevents the release of the naturally occurring melatonin. One tip is ensuring the room is blackened to limit exposure to natural light at the end of the shift. Power naps are also a useful supplement.

Take a power nap

A power nap is one way to fight fatigue and recharge during the day. It is best taken during our lowest level of alertness, which is usually around 2 pm or 3 pm. A duration of around 15 to 30 minutes is needed for it to be effective as if we take any more time than this our body enters into its usual sleep cycle. Once we are in normal sleep cycle, if we fail to complete it we can get what's called sleep inertia and end up feeling groggy, disoriented and even more sleepy that before.

Prepare for a good night's sleep

Develop a sleep routine: Go to bed and get up at the same time each day, allowing yourself 8 to 9 hours sleep a night. Keep this constant on weekends and days off. Initially you may miss your sleep-in, but you will adjust once you are getting the right amount of sleep.

Use your bed only for sleeping: Refrain from reading or watching TV in bed. If you can't sleep get out of bed and go into another room to do something relaxing until you feel tired again.

Get comfortable: Have a warm bath to make yourself feel relaxed and sleepy. Change into loose, comfortable clothing.

Relax your mind: Write down all you need to do the next day so that you can put these thoughts aside for the next day. If you wake up during the night worrying about work, write down what you need to remember before trying to go back to sleep. This helps you to put aside the need to remember things for the morning.

Exercise: Use regular exercise to improve sleep but be mindful that engaging in this less than three hours before bedtime can prevent sleepiness as the body is in a stimulated state. If you find you are mentally exhausted from work exercise will help you become physically tired as well and assist in achieving a better night's sleep.

Avoid stimulants: Caffeine drinks before bedtime can cause insomnia and can have a diuretic effect, meaning your sleep will be disturbed when you have to get up. Caffeine is found not just in coffee but also tea, hot chocolate, cocoa, cola and energy drinks. Alcohol is also one of the most commonly used sleeping aids. While an alcoholic drink before bedtime tends to help us go to sleep faster, it is metabolised at the rate of one standard drink per hour. This means that when all the alcohol has worn off you suffer withdrawal effects, with symptoms such as shallow and disrupted sleep, increased dream recall, nightmares, sweating, and a faster heart rate. Alcohol also inhibits REM sleep, which is important for memory consolidation.

Avoid eating late meals: The timing of when you eat affects your sleepiness. The time it takes for you to fall asleep is greater after a meal than it is one and a half hours after a meal, so the scheduling of your evening meal makes a difference.

Use relaxation techniques

When we summon up a picture of ourselves relaxing, we generally imagine lying or sitting somewhere peaceful — perhaps on a beach, in a park or in bed. There are a variety of techniques, however, that you can use while you are at work that do not need a quiet place to lie or sit. A selection of some quick, easy-to-do activities are outlined below. If you are feeling tense you can use one or two of these regularly during the day to release tension and improve your focus. With practice you can mediate wherever you are — at your desk, on the bus or even at a boring meeting or presentation!

BOUNCE-BACK ACTIVITY

Sleep check

Do you get enough sleep? Review the following statements to find out. The more they are true for you the more likely it is that you are not getting enough sleep.

▪ I often fall asleep watching television.

▪ I struggle to get out of bed in the morning.

▪ I often sleep in on the weekends.

▪ I have trouble with focus and memory.

▪ I often need a nap to make it through the day.

▪ I need an alarm clock to wake up.

▪ I feel tired, irritable and stressed during the day.

Body scan

Sit comfortably with your eyes closed. Focus on the toes of one foot and move your attention slowly up that leg, then slowly up your other leg, your torso, each arm, your neck and head. Notice the sensations that are present with openness and curiosity, but without trying to change them.

If you find your mind wanders, which is usual, just notice this and gently return your attention to your body.

Sitting meditation

Sit comfortably. Close your eyes, or if you can't do this, gaze downward. Direct your attention to your breathing. Should your mind wander off, which may occur frequently, gently return your attention to your breathing. If you feel like moving to make your-self more comfortable, then observe, with acceptance, the sensation that brought this to mind. When you do choose to move, do this with full awareness of the movement. Next you may wish to observe sounds in the environment without judging them. Then you may wish to shift your attention to observing your thoughts and emotions without judging them. Over time you should be able to do this for longer periods of time.

Mini relaxation techniques

Tension is who you think you should be. Relaxation is who you are.

Chinese proverb

These mini exercises are perfect for calming yourself in any place and at any time. You could use them, for example, when preparing to walk into a difficult meeting, or before responding to something that has upset you.

Breath control: Calm yourself by slowing and focusing on your breathing. Do this by breathing out with a sigh, breathing in deeply, and then holding your breath for a moment. Finally breathe out slowly and steadily.

Shoulder stretch: Breathe in and pull your shoulders upwards, then hold your breath and gently pull them back. Breathe out with a sigh, letting your shoulders drop down slowly as you do.

Tips for a developing headache

When you feel a headache developing, push on the pressure points on both temples and under the eyebrows at either side of the nose. Also press the centre of the base of the skull and the centre of the forehead.

If you are prone to severe headaches or migraines meditation or a relaxation exercise can sometimes delay onset when you sense the symptoms are appearing.

Practise mindfulness

> *For fast-acting relief, try slowing down.*
>
> Lily Tomlin

Being in the moment has almost become an art with today's pace of life. As we learn to work simultaneously on multiple tasks while dealing with interruptions and background noises, it is increasingly hard to focus on what we are doing. We tend to be less attentive to what is happening around us and act and interact automatically, without thinking. Sometimes this means we even miss opportunities that present.

While we may pride ourselves in our capacity to multi-task, we know that the brain is not wired to work productively in this way. How often in a day are you working on one or two tasks simultaneously while planning or worrying about something else? Are you finding it increasingly difficult to work on tasks requiring sustained concentration? Do you often work on automatic pilot, missing some of what is happening around you? If the answer is 'yes' then practice in mindfulness may help you work more effectively and with less stress.

The practice of mindfulness has become increasingly popular in helping busy people live in the moment. It comes from meditation principles used in Eastern spiritual practices, mainly within Buddhism. It involves being attentive to, and aware of, what is taking place in the present moment. Another activity that is simple but not easy.

How mindful are you?

Being mindful is staying open to the experience of the moment. Assess your level of mindfulness by considering how many of the following descriptors are typical of you.

- I am often running on automatic and not focusing on what I am doing.
- I often partly listen to people as I have other things on my mind.

- I often arrive at a destination without recall of the journey.
- When eating, I often do not notice what I just ate.
- I rush through things without being attentive to what I am doing.
- I tend to think about what I need to do next rather than what I am doing now.
- I often think of how things went in the past when I am doing something.
- I drop or spill things because I am not concentrating on what I am doing.
- I tend to be unaware of mild personal discomfort or tension.

The more these statements describe you, the more mindfulness practice may assist. Some exercises that can be used every day are outlined here.

Practise mindfulness in everyday activities

While meditation generally involves focusing on one thing, such as a breath, mindfulness focuses on the flow of an experience.

To be in the moment you need to attend to all of your senses: seeing, smelling, hearing, feeling and, if possible, tasting, whatever you are doing. This takes persistence and practice to be effective.

A good way of honing your skills is practising mindfulness in routine activities such as eating and walking. This provides an opportunity to engage mindfully in activities that may often be done on 'automatic pilot' or without awareness. It's all part of the slowing down of busyness.

Eating mindfully

Take a piece of food and look at with interest and curiosity as if you have never seen it before. Slowly explore what it looks like, its texture and colour. Then notice how it sounds as you press it gently. Take in its aroma. Notice your body movements as you place it in your mouth. Notice how it feels in your mouth, its taste. Notice the movements of your mouth as you chew it and swallow it. As thoughts and emotions arise while you are doing this notice these without judging them and return your attention to the food and the sensations of eating it.

You will find this experience of eating mindfully is very different to the typical experience of eating when your attention is focused elsewhere and you are not truly tasting the food. Try eating your lunch in this way on a busy day as a means of slowing down and practising mindfulness.

Walking mindfully

Generally when we are walking around we are thinking of other things, perhaps what we are going to say when we get there or the next task to be done. Practise walking slowly across a room and back, attending to the sensations of your body while you are doing this. Look directly ahead and notice what it looks, feels and sounds like as you walk. Should any thoughts or emotions occur, simply bring your attention back to the sensation of walking. The aim is to ensure your attention is not on reaching a destination, but on the sensation of walking.

You can apply this to any physical movement such as climbing stairs or photocopying. It is an excellent way of ensuring that exercise offers mental as well as physical benefit.

Closely connected to mindfulness is the concept of savouring. Usually associated with food, savouring involves getting the most out of pleasant experiences. Chapter 7 explores tips on how we can best savour moments.

Interacting mindfully

Using mindfulness when interacting and communicating with others is one way of being what is sometimes called 'authentically present'. Here are some tips on how to interact in this way:

• Be fully there with the person. Sit or stand facing them, maintaining good eye contact and ensuring open body posture.

- Avoid urgent moves such as a hand on the door, eyes on your watch, or a glance at the computer screen, as these suggest something or someone else is more important. If you are in a hurry and have limited time, state that you are happy to share a short time — not that you can only spare a short time. If the time available is insufficient, make an offer of more time later. For example: 'I have 10 minutes now to discuss it or if that is not enough for you let's make another time' rather than 'I've only got 10 minutes to spare'.

- Use empathy. Reflect back what people are feeling and show you care about them. Listen to the emotion and name it matter of factly; for example: 'It sounds like you are pretty frustrated …'

- Listen fully before responding. Do not predetermine the answer.

Being able to sit back, reflect and respond intentionally rather than react enhances both our quality of communication and the choices we make. Observing the moment dispassionately allows us to suspend our own beliefs and judgment. The space created means we can recognise our assumptions and emotional reactions and suspend our own opinions. The end result is authentic communication. People feel heard and understood, and we have usually developed a deeper appreciation of the situation.

Interestingly, the word 'authenticity' is increasingly appearing in the jargon of organisations, reflecting a focus on the need to be real and consistent in behaviour and values.

Get into flow

Have you ever been so in the moment that you have lost sense of time? Athletes often do, and call the experience 'being in the zone'. Commonly, people describe this as a state when time has stopped and you are immersed and totally absorbed in what you are doing. Psychologist Mike Csikszentmihalyi describes this

> ### BOUNCE-BACK ACTIVITY
>
> ## 'Me' diary
>
> Buy a notebook or diary and label it 'Me'. Each evening reflect on what you have done that day, to invest in your own self-care and resilience. Perhaps it was taking a break for lunch, reframing an issue, saying 'no' to additional work, or making time to relax. Be sure only to record what you are pleased with and what has worked well. Record the positive steps you have taken, regardless of how small they may seem.
>
> Reflecting back weekly over the diary will help you build confidence in your progress and give you a sense of how far you have come. On days where you believe you have nothing positive to write, consider what you may have done to maintain the status quo rather than regress.
>
> Over time, the diary will provide evidence to convince you of your success in moving forwards.

phenomenon as 'flow', and has spent many years investigating its benefits and how to achieve it.

According to Csikszentmihalyi a state of flow occurs when the challenges we face perfectly mesh with our abilities to meet them. For some of us it occurs with activities associated with the mind, such as reading an absorbing book or a challenging game of chess; for others it is associated with physicality, such as sport or dancing. There is also an impact on our psychological wellbeing.[1] He has also found that people are happier when they are in flow than when engaged in passive activity such as watching TV, or having nothing to do.

While a wide variety of activities lend themselves to flow they all comprise some of the following core elements:

• challenge, involving a degree of effort

- skill with a need for a level of personal capability
- a need for concentration
- clear goals with understanding of what needs to be done
- capacity for immediate feedback on how you are performing
- potential for deep, effortless involvement
- a sense of personal control over the task.

Work provides us with prime opportunity for flow, as unlike leisure it builds many of the conditions of flow into itself. There are usually clear goals and rules of performance and frequent feedback about how well or poorly we are doing. Work usually encourages concentration and minimises distractions, and often matches task difficulties to our talents and even our strengths. These all promote potential for engagement and immersion in what we are doing.

Finding activities that promote flow at work will heighten your personal satisfaction in your performance.

Chapter 5: Tips for rejuvenating the body

▌ Put in place strategies to prepare for and get a good night's sleep.

▌ Use mini relaxation techniques at work to reduce tension and enhance focus.

▌ Practise mindfulness. Be fully in the moment in all you do: eating, walking, interacting, and any activity.

▌ Find workplace activities that allow you to get into 'flow'.

▌ Use authentic presence when interacting with others. Be fully in the moment.

▌ Start a 'me' diary to build personal confidence in your progress in building resilience.

Channelling emotional energy: Achieving emotional balance

Managing and channelling our emotional energy is integral to building resilience. Emotions are extraordinarily powerful. They not only drive our energy, they also contain our history, experiences and understanding. Despite this, in western culture they are often not trusted and sometimes seen as a source of vulnerability and weakness. This chapter explores the impact of emotion at work, and provides techniques to manage negative feelings and harness the power of intuition.

Emotion at work

Workplaces have traditionally been emotion-free zones with much of the language of business focused on the rational. Using emotion has often been confused with being emotional. Typical statements such as 'Let's not let emotion cloud our judgment' or 'Let's focus on facts not feelings' have made it less legitimate to talk about emotions. This focus on intellectual functioning is often at the expense of considering the emotional content of an experience. We know that emotions are an integral part of our human nature. Simply trying to ignore or suppress them does not work. They continue to impact on us, and not managing them can derail our performance.

When we get upset in our job the sources most typically stem from:

- how much we feel appreciated and valued in what we do
- our sense of belonging and connection with others
- the independence and autonomy we are given to make decisions for ourselves
- our status and standing in relation to those we work with
- the role we have, its label, and the activities we do as part of it.

Consider the last time you or your colleagues were upset and which one of these was true for you at the time, and triggered a reaction.

Identifying and addressing these concerns, both personally and within teams, can both improve relationships and increase trust. Teams and leaders that create an environment where these issues are regularly considered decrease the capacity for negative conflict and discontent.

Emotional intelligence

A significant development relating to emotions has been the concept of emotional intelligence and its measurement, emotional quotient (EQ).[1] Recognition that managing emotion is important to job performance, together with the capacity to measure this via EQ testing, seems to have added legitimacy to discussing emotion in the workplace. High EQ, like its counterpart intelligence quotient (IQ), is now seen as a critical asset in many jobs. Programs on EQ development are commonplace, especially for leaders, and sometimes emotional intelligence is used as a criteria in staff selection.

Emotionally intelligent people are better able to monitor their own and other's feelings, understand them, and use this information to guide how they respond.

While definitions of emotional intelligence vary and will not be explored here, many of its elements are integral to achieving emotional balance.

Emotional labour

Emotional resilience is especially important if you hold a job that has a high degree of what is known as emotional labour or emotion work.[2] This is the work required to manage your emotions in a way that makes them consistent with what your employer expects.

If you are a waitress, for example, you are expected to smile and treat customers positively, while if you work in debt collection you need to provoke a degree of anxiety. Similarly, if you are a nurse, you are expected to be warm and empathetic in difficult situations involving sickness, trauma and death. All of these jobs require you to display certain emotions, regardless of how you are actually feeling at the time.

Presenting the required public image means either faking it or modifying how you feel. Both involve energy and labour.

Interestingly, many jobs with high emotional labour are not well rewarded. Call centre operators, front-of-business staff and childcare workers are all good examples of this. It seems that the emotional demands of occupations remain overlooked, with wages being more closely related to the intellectual requirements of the job.

Added to less remuneration, there is a growing body of evidence that emotional labour may also lead to burnout over time. This means developing emotional resilience is even more critical if your job is high in emotional work.

Emotion and energy

Emotions are a source of energy. They move us to take action. At their height they create exhilaration and motivation, while at their depths incapacity and despair. The stronger the emotion, the greater the energy it provides.

The secret is being able to use and channel negative emotions positively. For example, you can use disappointment as a motivator to try harder, or use the energy of your anger to rise above an issue. When jockey Damian Oliver won the Melbourne Cup there wasn't a dry eye in the house as a nation saw him channel the grief of losing his brother into victory. Negative emotion also promotes focus and rationale thinking. This means that a low mood has its advantages at work, in situations of risk assessment, detailed analysis and sustained concentration.

This chapter provides an overview of building resilience through managing negative emotions, while Chapter 7 explores ways of evoking positivity.

Channel negative energy positively
Tune into your emotions

The first step in learning to manage emotions is to understand the richness and complexity of the feelings we can experience. This is not always easy as sometimes emotions are very subtle, while at other times they offer strong, conflicting feelings. If we are grieving, for example, we may be confused at experiencing despair and anger simultaneously. If we are happy our elation can be tinged with sadness, perhaps because a significant person is missing or because of the costs of success.

The eight central emotions are joy, acceptance, fear, surprise, sadness, disgust, anger and anticipation. However, for each of these core emotions there are hundreds of variations in intensity. Understanding which emotion we are personally feeling is a key aspect of emotional resilience. When we feel let down, for example, is it frustration, rejection or dismay we are experiencing? Identifying the actual emotion allows us to make a more informed response.

Some people seem to have greater self-awareness when it comes to recognising personal emotions. You can check out how you rate by completing the Emotional Self-Awareness Checklist below.

If you believe this is an area of development for you, a simple way to improve your emotional awareness is to re-experience a past emotional event in your mind and notice the physiological response evoked. To demonstrate, close your eyes and recall mentally a time when you felt angry. Spend a few minutes recreating the scene in your mind and notice how it feels. Some people feel their jaw tense; others feel the stomach or chest tighten, or breathing deepen. Everybody is different. Identifying the bodily response you have can help you understand what various emotions feel like physically for you and allow you to better tune into your emotions before they become overwhelming. A useful tip when recreating negative emotions, however, is to shake off

---

BOUNCE-BACK ACTIVITY

Emotional Self-Awareness Checklist

Consider which of the following items are true for you:

▌ I can name my own emotions.
▌ I feel different emotions at the same time.
▌ I am aware of the emotion I am feeling at present.
▌ I am able to sit with an emotion without acting on it.
▌ I can channel emotional energy into positive action.
▌ I am able to reflect on and learn from my emotional experiences.

Score one point for each question you agreed with. The higher your score, the more emotionally self-aware you may be.

the emotion afterwards, or follow the mental image of a negative experience with one of joy.

Notice when you do this how easy it is to recreate the intensity of past emotions. This demonstrates the unconscious power of our emotional history. Ways on how to use positive past experiences to your advantage are explored later in the chapter.

Choose your mood

I think therefore I am — Descartes

At work we are responsible for our own mood. While we will all have personal problems and ups and downs at some time in our lives, our colleagues will only be empathetic for a short time. Being down or negative for extended periods causes tension in teams and impacts on others' wellbeing. Given the time we spend with others at work, being frequently negative is not acceptable or fair to our co-workers.

Using the power of self-talk can help you to start to shift your mood and bring your emotions under control. As explained in Chapter 3, this involves attending to the voice in your head and modifying what you are saying to yourself.

Here are some typical examples of using self-talk to change your mood:

- 'I'll never get this done' becomes 'Just focus on one thing at a time.' This changes anxiety and panic to calmness and focus.
- 'Here we go again with another day of difficult customers' becomes 'Each customer is a different challenge. I'll see if I can sort out their issues quickly today.' This can change apathy or dismay and disengagement to hope and increased motivation.

When you change your self-talk you will also need to make the corresponding shift in body language and actions. Making positive statements while grimacing or sitting tensely will not be effective. Neither will telling yourself to get onto tasks without actually doing this. Taking positive action consolidates the mood shift. Acting confidently whenever you feel nervous, for example, builds confidence. It's a case of 'fake it until you make it'.

The next time you are in a negative mood, tune into your self-talk and actively practise changing it and acting accordingly. Notice the impact.

Understand the impact of pressure

Management of our mood is undoubtedly more of a challenge when we are under pressure. Any bad traits that we have intensify. If we have a tendency to be intolerant we can become very intolerant; if we are slightly critical we don't hold back in our opinion. Unfortunately, our strengths can also undo us. We may pride ourselves in being highly organised but may turn into a 'control freak' or micro manager when stressed. If we are well known for our analytical skills we may overdo this and develop 'analysis paralysis'.

We are said to have a dark side of our personality that can emerge when we are stressed or not held accountable for our behaviour.[3] This can have particularly devastating results if we are in a senior leadership position. Knowing your personality and how it changes under pressure can assist you manage your mood. If you are unsure of the characteristics you display when stressed ask your partner or co-worker — they are sure to know!

Recognise the impact of physical factors

It is easy to underestimate the impact hormones and tiredness have on our mood and energy. We often search for reasons behind our reaction or outburst. Non-cooperative co-workers, a demanding boss, or a traffic jam on the way to work are typical excuses we may offer.

However, our emotional state can also be a product of tiredness as we know that we are more fragile and likely to overact when we are tired. Less overtly acknowledged is the impact of hormonal changes, especially at work. Menopause or pregnancy, for example, can produce long periods where our normal moods are altered. Self-management is a particular challenge during these times, especially when we either do not recognise this, or we accept it as the way we now are. Strategies such as self-talk will not have the same impact in these situations, and medical advice may be needed.

When it comes to these physical sources of mood we really need to work more on strategies for our body rather than our mind. The ideas in Chapters 2 and 3 in building physical endurance are of most benefit here.

Use positive memories to lift mood

A simple mood booster that you can do anywhere is recalling past happy experiences. As explained earlier in this chapter, taking yourself back in your mind to an enjoyable or joyful event can help you bring an element of that positivity to the present moment. Most of us have experienced feeling upset or even crying when we have recalled a traumatic event. You can use this power of recall in a positive way by focusing on happy times and bringing past joy to the present.

To do this, close your eyes and visualise your chosen event. Use all your senses to recall the experience. See it, smell it, hear it, and finally feel the emotions associated with it. Then bring this feeling back to where you are sitting. Our emotional history is stored subconsciously and we can put it to good use at any time with a little attention and focus.

If your mood is low this simple visualisation may help.

Control powerful emotions

Managing strong feelings and impulses is an important part of emotional resilience. In reality, it is not the emotion, but the action we take when we feel it that makes the difference. When our anger produces aggression it is unhelpful as the situation that led to it often remains unresolved, and people around us are more likely to avoid us. When the anger is directed towards problem-solving it becomes instead a useful motivating force. In this way learning how to manage and channel negative emotion can add value to our lives.

Can we control powerful emotions?

Brain research has demonstrated that while an emotional response may be activated automatically we have the means to intervene and control it.

Our emotional experiences generate from two areas of the brain. The automatic emotional responses come from a small almond shaped area deep in the brain called the amygdala. This allows us to make rapid responses to threats in the environment without having to think about it. While very effective when we need to respond to hazardous situations in the shortest possible time, it is not useful when we need to control our response. In contrast, the control of our emotional responses sits in the prefrontal cortex at the front of our brain.

Both of these emotion-related areas — the amygdala and prefrontal cortex — feed into each other and interact. Because how we evaluate what is happening is processed in the prefrontal cortex, this affects our response. For example, if we see another person get angry, we may think that that is just how they are and not take much notice, or we may think that we are under threat and feel increased distress. This means that the prefrontal cortex, through its feedback to the amygdala response, plays an essential role in whether an emotional response is inflamed or reduced.

However, controlling emotions should not be confused with suppressing them. Suppression is not healthy as this can produce depression or self-destructive behaviours.

Respond rather than react

When we communicate impulsively, we are said to be reacting rather than responding. In these situations it is as though we are being forced to act in that way, with someone or something else being the cause of our outburst. In contrast, when we respond thoughtfully we behave in a way that leaves us feeling in control.

Reactions commonly stem from feelings of being overwhelmed, stressed, scared, outraged, hurt, agitated, frustrated, angry, sad, disappointed, or anxious. These feelings cause us to lash out verbally or physically, cry, blame others, withdraw, or resort to tantrums. This behaviour may sometimes offer short-term rewards. Getting angry, for example, may get us noticed, let us vent frustration, or manipulate others. It may also increase our chances of getting our own way. Often this pay-off can reinforce our behaviour, although in the long term this ultimately destroys relationships.

When working with a team, a lack of emotional regulation can have an impact on respectful relationships, and ultimately on culture, as people guard against risking a reaction from colleagues.

Use the Reaction Checklist on the opposite page to determine if you have a tendency to react.

Know your buttons

When incidents trigger a reaction we often refer to this as 'pushing our buttons'. Knowing your 'buttons' is one way to help you control your emotions.

Commonly our 'buttons' are pressed when we feel our values or principles are being violated, or when we feel that some aspect of ourselves is being attacked, or when our personal relationships are under threat. Identifying the triggers behind your reaction assists you to anticipate and adjust your response.

One way to identify your triggers is to reflect on situations where you have had a strong negative reaction. Chances are you may have felt the outburst was justified at the time, but on reflection you think it would have been better to have been less irrational.

BOUNCE-BACK ACTIVITY

Reaction Checklist

Read through the behaviours below and identify those that are true to you.

▮ When someone criticises me I tend to take it personally.

▮ When there are problems at work I react first and problem-solve later.

▮ When I experience strong emotions, I find it hard to get back on task in the short term.

▮ I find it difficult to stay calm in pressured situations.

▮ Sometimes I feel that my emotions have overtaken the situation.

▮ I look to external causes when I am distressed.

▮ Relationships with others have been affected by my reactions.

Score one point for each question. The higher your score the more likely that you are able to react rather than respond to situations.

Try to recall what you thought, felt and did in the situation. What was it about that situation that really created the outburst? What buttons were pressed?

Now imagine the situation as it would have been if you were in control of your emotions. What would you think, feel and do in this new situation? How does this differ from the previous scenario?

Follow up by reading through 'Bounce back: Reflecting on reactions' on the following page, and use it on a daily basis for a while to learn more about yourself and understand how you can change your reactions to persons or situations at work and at home.

BOUNCE-BACK ACTIVITY

Reflecting on reactions

The next time you react instead of respond at work or at home ask yourself:

▪ *Why am I feeling like this?*
What triggered this response? Which of my 'buttons' have been pressed?

▪ *What is my contribution to this?*
Often when we react rather than respond, the response tells us as much about ourselves as the other person or the situation. What is it about you that is making this happen? What personal concerns or fears have triggered the reaction? Perhaps you are reading things into the situation and this is the real source of the emotional reaction. Are you feeling rejected, not respected or devalued? Ask yourself: 'What are the payoffs for me of reacting this way?'

▪ *What do I want to change?*
Listen to your emotions. What do you really want to happen? What are your needs in this situation?

▪ *Whose problem is this really?*
How much of the problem belongs to you, how much to others? Whose responsibility is it?

▪ *What next?*
How does this reflection change next actions and future responses?

De-stress after difficult encounters

Does your job involve dealing with emotionally charged and difficult situations? If so, this can have a cumulative effect on your wellbeing if encounters are not dealt with as they arise. Angry customers, distressed clients or sharing of traumatic experiences all have an impact on our personal health.

Wherever possible, it is important to de-stress after each gruelling incident. This can prove challenging in many workplaces as often there is an expectation that you continue to work on the counter, on the telephone line, or in providing service delivery.

Listed in the box below, De-stressing Techniques, are some de-stressing techniques commonly used at work. Choose the ones that will work best for you and try to use them after emotional incidents. Everybody is different, and what works for you may not work for your colleagues.

If you are a team leader, part of your role is to provide a safe place for people to vent and 'get things off their chest'. Sometimes it can be hard to determine if a person simply wants to vent or if they are looking for action on an issue. A simple way of clarifying this is asking: 'Were you wanting me to do anything about this or are you just sharing what has happened?' Many times a person will say that they realise there is no resolution but it makes them feel better just to talk about it. This

---

De-stressing Techniques

Distract yourself by absorbing yourself in another task.

Escape by going for a quick walk, grabbing a coffee, or visiting another area to pick up or drop off an item.

Gain support from others. Talk with co-workers about what happened, gain their perspective, or share a joke about it.

Write down or type your thoughts about the event and then put them aside.

Change your self-talk and the way you view the episode, as described in Chapter 3.

Use the mini relaxation techniques in Chapter 5 to reduce tension.

Vent your frustration and de-brief with a trusted colleague, your mentor or supervisor.

decreases the pressure on you as a leader to problem-solve. For self-sufficient people who do not want the matter to go any further, this approach also allows them to maintain their need to self-manage the situation.

Professions where there is high risk of vicarious trauma such as social work, emergency work and psychology adopt professional debriefing or mentoring as an integral part of their work. This is essential practice for any work that is emotionally demanding. More about the importance of emotional support at work is explored in Chapter 7.

Emotion in decision-making

Emotions influence our decision-making. We know this through documented cases of people who have suffered damage to the limbic section of their brain. These people have normal intellectual functioning but struggle with simple decision-making. While they can think and analyse perfectly they are unable to act appropriately or make effective decisions.

There is substantial evidence that human beings developed a sophisticated emotional system long before the intellect, as we know it today developed. Neglect and suppression of emotional processing over generations has meant we have lost this. Today when we talk about emotional information we typically describe it as instinct or intuition.

Use your intuition

Trust your gut.

Donald Trump's advice in his TV series *The Apprentice*

Do you sometimes get an intuitive hunch or gut instinct at work? Do you ignore it or go with it? Intuition is the ability to sense messages from our internal store of emotional memory. It is thought to be the remnant of an essential warning system for danger that was critical to our ancestors for survival. Today it lives on when we sense apprehension, uncertainty or a sense of danger without conscious knowledge of why.

Using the power of intuition is not about rejecting common sense and logic but adding another dimension to good judgment. It provides a 'red flag', indicating that issues need further exploration. At work, if you have a flash of intuition on a topic where you have considerable experience this instinct is more likely to be an unconscious analysis of all you know. It reflects all of your principles and insights and deserves further investigation.

Studies into intuitive decision-making show it plays its biggest role at work in people-related situations such as selection, marketing, identifying potential partners and networks, or identifying political motives. It has also been discovered that we tend to use it more when time and information is limited, when we are panicking, or when we are in a positive mood. Complex situations lend well to using intuitive judgment, as analysis of all of the information may be overwhelming or impossible. Wiseman's study into what makes people lucky, described in Chapter 3, also found trusting intuition was a key principle of luck.

There are lots of ways of capitalising on the value of intuition at work. Try out some of these tips.

- Use silence to tap into your intuition. It is in our quiet moments and when we are calm that we have intuitive breakthroughs. Pay attention to your inner voice and the deeper information it conveys.

- Recognise the role of intuition in creativity and inspiration. Foster it in others.

- Respect the language of intuition. Do not dismiss it because it presents as images, symbols, impressions and sensations that make no logical sense.

- Suspend judgment. Intuition adds to good judgment; it does not replace it. But if we let judgment intercede too soon it prevents insight.

- Use longer than usual pauses during conversation.
- Voice your intuition. State what you sense, feel, or have a hunch about.
- Explore others' intuition. Ask questions such as 'How do you feel? What do you sense? What's your intuition on this? Are we missing something here?'

Emotion in relationship-building

Recognising and managing our emotions is essential in relationship building. We connect with others not because of who they are but because of how they make us feel. The glue is emotion. Many of the strategies in creating positive energy explored in the next chapter will promote good working relationships.

We also need to manage negativity in our interactions with others. This does not mean avoiding being critical. High-performing teams value critique and challenge as an important way of focusing on continuous improvement. What is important is that criticism is managed in a respectful and constructive way.

Manage conflicts early

Even in the most cohesive teams interpersonal conflict beyond differences in opinion can occur. If you experience this, the secret here is to resolve it early to stop it escalating. What starts as a small misunderstanding can move into assumptions and then fixed opinions about others and eventually to a breakdown of any type of constructive communication. Unresolved conflict takes up unnecessary nervous energy and can have a major impact on your emotional health as well as broader team dynamics.

As a first step, recognise your part in the conflict. What impact are your needs, moods, values or personal style having on the relationship? The questions in the Bounce Back activity on reflecting on reactions earlier in the chapter may be of relevance. Determine what you can personally change to resolve the situation, and whether this is viable for you.

Often in the early stages of conflict, providing open and honest feedback in a constructive way will resolve it. While this sounds easy, many people feel uncomfortable providing feedback that co-workers may not want to hear. The most common excuses we make for this are:

- 'We haven't had the time or opportunity to talk about it.'

- 'It's not our job to say anything.'

- 'We are worried about retaliation or loss of friendship.'

Skill in giving feedback can only be developed through practice. Basic guidelines are:

- Focus on specific behaviour and not personality attributes or characteristics that people cannot change.

- Provide the feedback privately and in a timely way. As soon as possible after the event is preferable, allowing for privacy.

- Discuss the issue as a shared problem. For example, ask: 'What can *we* do about this?'

- Collaboratively develop options.

- Ask for, and be open to acting on, the other person's perspective.

Chapter 6: Tips for channelling emotional energy

■ Understand the importance of managing emotion in the workplace.

■ Invest more in emotional resilience if your job is high in emotional labour.

■ Improve emotional self-awareness by tuning into your feelings.

■ Recognise changes in your personality traits when under pressure.

■ Choose your mood, using self-talk or positive memory recall.

■ Know your buttons, and reflect on when you react rather than respond.

■ Use de-stressing techniques after difficult encounters at work, and support others in this process.

■ Tap into your intuition and increase the value placed on this in personal and team decision-making.

■ Resolve interpersonal conflicts early to stop them escalating.

Creating positivity:
More on emotional resilience

The benefits of positive emotion

Workplaces often emphasise how to manage negative behaviour rather than foster positive interaction and energy. Typically, we have codes of conduct, protocols and human resource processes to deal with deviation from expected behaviours, without the equivalent energy being spent on creating a positive work environment.

We know, however, that emotion is contagious, and we catch and feel the emotions around us. In a team, positivity builds on itself and improves relationships and productivity. Spending time with uplifting people is a useful strategy when you are feeling low as it can boost your own mood.

On a personal level, a positive mood makes us more open to exploring solutions and enhances creativity. There are also advantages to our psychological wellbeing as positivity hastens recovery from stress. All this adds to building our emotional balance.

Our customers also benefit. Research shows that positive interactions such as smiling and friendliness mean clients are more likely to return, recommend your organisation, and more highly rate your service.

This chapter focuses on ways of developing and promoting positive emotion.

Communicate positively

Happiness never decreases by being shared.

Buddha

How positive are you seen by others? Positive people are open and approachable, with obvious energy and enthusiasm. Their company is motivating as they focus on possibility rather than negativity.[1] It's not that they do not have problems; it's just that they choose not to spend time talking about them. In reality, when people ask 'How are you?' they are being polite and do not actually want your full medical history. In a team, colleagues will be empathetic initially but will tire of continually hearing about difficulties you are having at work or at home.

Use the Checklist for Positive Communication below to determine how positive you or your colleagues are in your communication.

Checklist for Positive Communication

Positive communicators are more likely to:
- spend more time talking about the good things that are happening
- actively appreciate the efforts of others
- enthusiastically share thoughts and plans for the future
- have a solution orientation to problems
- value and respect other people's points of view
- communicate in an open and honest yet constructive way
- take the opportunity to spend time talking about enjoyable activities they are involved in
- be open to new ideas and thoughts

Express appreciation

Appreciation is a wonderful thing: It makes what is excellent in others belong to us as well.

Voltaire

Do you frequently thank others for their effort and contribution? Regardless of the job we hold we all like to feel appreciated and valued. Genuine appreciation not only improves our job satisfaction it also builds relationships.

The simplest and most powerful way of being appreciative is to provide direct feedback to others, either privately or publicly. A positive genuine comment from a colleague or our manager can mean the difference between feeling the day has been useful or stressful. When, for example, somebody says 'Thanks so much for backing me up today I was feeling pretty anxious before you stepped in to help', you can feel it was a day well spent.

To maximise the impact of your feedback makes sure it is personal, timely and addresses the specific actions done rather than just offering a general 'Well done'.

Show gratitude

Closely related to appreciating others is the concept of gratitude. Studies have shown that expressing gratitude makes us happier and creates a deeper connection with others. It works at a deeper level than expressing appreciation as it involves consciously thinking about what we are grateful for. The underlying rationale is that how we feel about our past depends entirely on our memories. Being grateful amplifies our good memories and therefore enhances positivity.[2]

A popular and effective activity for focusing on gratitude is 'Counting Your Blessings'. This bounce-back exercise, as described here, is especially helpful during difficult periods when we are more likely to be absorbed in what is off rather than on track.

> ### BOUNCE-BACK ACTIVITY
>
> ## Count your blessings
>
> Each evening take five minutes to reflect on up to five things that you are grateful for. These do not need to be outstanding events, rather everyday things, such as a word of thanks from another or getting a task done. Reviewing positive memories frequently helps us feel brighter and offers perspective. It also works towards making positive reflection part of our everyday thinking.

Be generous

For attractive lips, speak words of kindness.

Audrey Hepburn

Generosity of spirit builds teamwork. It's a case of anything is possible if nobody wants to take the credit. Unfortunately, ego and self-interest can sometimes create highly competitive environments where generosity towards colleagues is sidelined.

One commonly advocated activity to build a spirit of generosity is performing random acts of kindness — spontaneously helping somebody without any expectation of a reciprocation.

A study by Allan Luks of 3,000 volunteers found that performing this kind act not only makes you feel good it also improves your health. Volunteers in his study described a rush of euphoria followed by a longer period of calm after helping others. This triggering of endorphins after an act of altruism Luks termed 'helper's high'.[3]

At work, small acts of kindness, such as going out of your way to provide back-up are also tangible demonstrations of respect. Often when team relationships break down, common courtesies and simple acts of support are the first to disappear.

> ### BOUNCE-BACK ACTIVITY
>
> ## Let somebody else shine
>
> Select a member of your team whom you can let shine. Provide support and guidance in tasks and make sure they get public acknowledgement for their achievements. Do this quietly without others knowing and notice how good this makes you feel.

Try the power of a smile

You'll see the sun come shining through if you just smile.

Charlie Chaplin

The face we present to the world directly impacts on how others see us. Smiling is a biologically programmed response to something positive. It conveys warmth, approachability and friendliness. Smiling lets others know that we accept them and, in return, they accept us. This simple interaction on greeting can set the tone for the communication that follows.[4]

When we smile, even if we do not feel like it, our body registers its physical message. A number of research studies have shown that faking a facial expression produces the same effects on the body as a genuine emotion. In one study, for example, participants who mimicked a fearful expression had a corresponding increase in heart rate and skin temperature.

What this means is that just by smiling we can make ourselves feel better. One note of caution though: people judge genuine smiles as more likeable than fake attempts, so if you are faking positivity you need to adopt the corresponding body language.

Remember, communication depends 93% on our voice tone and body language and only 7% on the words and content. On the telephone it is our voice and its resonance and intonation that makes up 84% of our emotional influence.

Diplomats and politicians who have to greet and smile at people all day use what is known as the 'Easy Cheese Technique'. To practise this, say the words 'easy cheese' to yourself without opening your mouth. The result is a soft, natural looking, smile suitable for all occasions. There's no doubt that we all have days when we need the easy cheese approach!

Change posture

Just changing body posture can also make you feel better. If you are feeling upset, lifting your body upwards is very helpful. Looking down increases your internal focus. Stop and try this for a moment. Let your shoulders droop and look downwards. Note how you feel. Trying to feel positive in this stance is very difficult. Now, put your shoulders back and look upwards and try to feel negative. Just adopting a different posture can elevate your mood — this is an especially useful tip for times when you are feeling nervous, such as greeting a new client or making a request of your boss. Turning your eyes upwards instead of directly to the front is also very useful to stop you from crying.

BOUNCE-BACK ACTIVITY

Experimenting with a smile

Try smiling more over a period of a week and notice how you feel and its impact on your relationships with others. Notice if people respond differently and how this impacts on your interactions. Also, take note of how smiling lifts your mood?

Have fun

Laughter is a tranquiliser with no side effects.

Arnold Glasgow

Having fun at work seems to be a thing of the past. Whether it is workloads, concern about job security, or just a manager who frowns on any kind of frivolity, many people lament having far less fun than they used to.

Fun is good for us. We now know regular laughter produces biochemical and physiological changes in our body. Just check out the long list of benefits. Fun lowers blood pressure, relaxes muscles, improves our breathing, massages internal organs like our heart and lungs, boosts immunity, calms the nervous system, improves digestion, boosts mood, improves circulation, increases blood oxygenation, helps the body release the pleasure chemical dopamine and lowers heart rate ... and all of this free of charge while having a good time!

When we are stressed laughter also lowers levels of the stress hormones cortisol, adrenaline and noradrenalin and relieves anxiety and depression. If you are ill it can speed the healing process, relieve pain and reduce any work-related sickness by 50%.

Indeed, if we were able to bottle laughter we could throw away a lot of our medication.

In workplaces, laughter and humour — far from being a dis-traction from performance — can enhance it. This means pro-moting fun in the workplace can be serious business. One example is the FISH philosophy generated out of a film produced by John Christensen in 1998 of the famous Pike Place Fish Market in Seattle. This featured fishmongers who spent 12-hour shifts stacking, packing and selling fish in freezing conditions. The film showcased how gruelling work could be fun when people chose to:

- be there for colleagues and customers
- make someone's day

- choose their attitude, and finally
- play and have a laugh.

This approach, termed the 'FISH philosophy' has since been implemented in workplaces across the world.[5]

In what seems a contradiction to the spontaneity of fun, we sometimes need to plan and give permission for fun activities to happen at work. What have you done in the last month to bring a sense of fun to your workplace and what could you do? How can you build fun into daily interactions?

Give and receive support

We make a living by what we get. We make a life by what we give.

Winston Churchill

Caring and supportive relationships foster resilience. At work if we have relationships that create trust, provide role models, and offer encouragement this bolsters our rebound capacity.

Resilient people make and maintain connections with others. They have somebody to accept help from, but are also ready to offer such support. Encouraging social networks, together with formal support structures such as mentoring or coaching, are important in building emotional support.

For some of us, asking for, or taking the support offered, is not as easy as giving it. Are you guilty of being too independent or self-sufficient to accept help? Receiving support is not a weakness, and receiving it also fails to acknowledge the benefits others gain from giving. If you look at things from this perspective, refusing the assistance is rejecting the gift of kindness.

Effective teamwork involves give and take, and balancing the needs of individuals and the team. Sometimes we have to suppress our own needs for the welfare of the team overall. Being supportive is generally acknowledged as a key characteristic of a good leader and team member.[6]

> ## BOUNCE-BACK ACTIVITY
>
> ### Be a good teammate
>
> Psychologist Chris Peterson developed this exercise as a way of promoting support and kindness within teams. Practise the following behaviours with your own team. Keep track of what you did and how it made you feel.
>
> ▮ Be fully present
>
> ▮ Don't complain or feel jealous.
>
> ▮ Do more than your share.
>
> ▮ Volunteer without being promoted.
>
> ▮ Spread praise.
>
> ▮ Help the leaders and group meet their goals.

Savour the good times

Savouring, by relishing and paying attention to something enjoyable, is another proven way of lifting mood. While we tend to think about savouring in relation to eating our favourite foods, studies have shown savouring the positive aspects of daily life improves our health and happiness.[7]

We can translate this to the workplace by savouring accomplishments such as completing a project, being a mentor, or through routine aspects of our work that give us pleasure, such as helping customers.

So, what do we need to do to savour an event at work or at home? Try the following tips.

During the event:

• Sharpen your perceptions of the event. Focus on certain elements and block out others. For example, when listening to an inspiring presentation, hone into the speaker's voice and presence and block out all other noises or sensations.

- Absorb yourself. Get totally immersed in the present or anticipated experience. Try not to think, just sense. Do not think
about what you need to do tomorrow or pick up on your
way home from work, concentrate only on what you are
doing there and then, and nothing else.

After the event:

- Share the experience with friends and colleagues by telling
them how much you enjoyed and valued it.
- Consciously build on the memory. Take a physical souvenir of
the event, such as a photograph or ipod recording and remi-
nisce about it later with others. You can also intentionally store
mental images, with the anticipation of returning to them at a
later date.
- Congratulate yourself. Tell yourself how impressed others are, and
remember how long you have waited for this to happen.
Remember, however, that lavishing praise quietly on yourself
may be more appropriate given the Australian norm of humility.

As with mindfulness — described in Chapter 5 — practising
savouring at home in everyday activities can help build these
skills. Savouring simple pleasures like enjoying food, sitting in the
garden or listening to music is a great way to start and will make
positive activities even more relaxing and enjoyable.

Chapter 7: Tips for creating positivity

▌ Exude positivity. Be approachable, enthusiastic and open to others' opinions and ideas.

▌ Express appreciation and recognise the efforts of others. Encourage a climate of this within your team.

▌ Show gratitude and count your blessings. Notice and reflect more on what is going well than what is not.

▌ Be generous and let others in your team shine.

▌ Use the power of a smile.

▌ Introduce a sense of fun in the workplace.

▌ Readily give support and accept it willingly from others.

▌ Lift your mood by savouring the good experiences you have.

Achieving purpose and meaning: Getting the soul right

He who has a 'why' to live, can bear with almost any 'how'.

Friedrich Nietzsche

Looking for purpose

Do you believe you have purpose in your life?

As human beings we seek a sense of value or meaning in what we do. We need to be connected to something beyond ourselves to give us a sense of worth. Investing in building this on a daily basis promotes resilience.

In western society we have seen a resurgence of spirituality as people increasingly seek purpose. Within Australia, while only around 15% of people attend church at least once a month, there are signs of growth in religious fundamentalism and non-traditional religious practice such as Buddhism. Anzac Day has become a spiritual day to many, and in a world that has increased communication but not necessarily connectiveness, people are desperate to belong.

Spirituality is often confused with religion but is much broader and does not necessarily involve a particular god or religious persuasion. Some people find a sense of meaning through their family, the communities they belong to or their work. Others try altruistic pursuits or activities involving citizenship or social consciousness.

So why are we experiencing this increased interest in a search for meaning?

In the western world part of this search seems to derive, in part, from disenchantment with materialism and the treadmill of life. The centre-stage held by capitalism and consumerism in our society is being challenged slowly. We want more meaning to our existence and ways of connecting with something larger than ourselves. Excitement around the election of Barack Obama as president of the United States reinforces how we are thirsting for leadership that embraces vision, values and moral commitment. The recent Global Financial Crisis has also placed spiritual capital firmly in view for workplaces, given its origins in self-focus, greed and a loss of moral commitment.

Avoiding affluenza

Money buys a better class of misery.

Spike Milligan

'Affluenza' is the term used to capture the need to strive for ever-increasing material wealth. A combination of the words 'affluence' and 'influenza', it describes the unfulfilled feeling we get in trying to keep up with the Joneses. It's a type of socially transmitted condition, with the symptoms being a dogged pursuit of owning and having more.

Our society generally measures success by fame, wealth, and status. At work this is salary, benefits, title and position. Buying into this popular notion of success can set us up for unnecessary disappointment.

Proponents of the term 'affluenza' believe valuing endless increases in material wealth lead to feelings of worthlessness and dissatisfaction rather than a happier life. When we acquire the DVD player, then we covet the plasma TV, and when we progress to that we aspire to the integrated home entertainment system. Each acquisition creates a personal need for something bigger and better. This pursuit of something better ironically leaves us more disenchanted than satisfied and may explain why after 50 years of economic growth in western society levels of happiness have not increased.

It's a sobering fact of life that many of us may never achieve our materialistic goals. Mostly they are a long way off, or when they are realised they only give us a brief moment of satisfaction.

An alternate to catching affluenza is to live according to our values as we can act on these at any moment and do not have to strive to acquire them. Several ideas on how you might do this are explored in the folllowing chapter.

The search for happiness

> *Happiness is someone to love, something to do and something to look forward to.*
>
> US psychiatrist, Gordon Livingston

In a similar way to catching affluenza we have been caught up in the pursuit of happiness. Throughout time, sages have offered advice on how to attain the perfect life. The drawback of this focus on being happy is that life is unpredictable, complex and not easily controlled. Resilience in our changing times needs an acceptance that setbacks are part of the richness of life, and it is unrealistic to expect to be happy all of the time.

What we need to learn is how to experience anxiety, fear and disappointment and convert this into positive action. As described in Chapter 1, resilience cannot be built without bouncing back from the tough times. It is the obstacles that not only teach us coping skills but give us a better appreciation of the good times.

The importance of spiritual belief

Spiritual belief provides many people with a sense of purpose in their lives. It can, however, offer benefits beyond this. If your spiritual practice promotes meditation or prayer, this improves mood and calmness; involvement in a community such as a church also offers a feeling of belonging. We know that those who are spiritually involved have a lower incidence of disease. All of these factors add to resilience.

Spirituality also incorporates a sense of being at peace with yourself and others. Achieving this combines the mindfulness and meditation explored in Chapter 3 with the acceptance and gratitude discussed in Chapter 5.

Interestingly, people who have survived trauma or life-threatening illness often become more spiritual. It's almost as though unforeseen events prompt a coming to terms with the fact that the world is not as just, safe and predictable as you may have thought it was. In these situations spiritualty can restore hope and create a more balanced view of what is really important. Reflect on any experiences you have had. Do you have friends or relatives who have reassessed priorities after a significant life event?

The Concept of Spiritual Quotient

In the same way that emotional intelligence can now be measured using emotional quotient (EQ), our level of spiritual intelligence can be measure using a spirituality quotient (SQ). Table 7 provides an indication of some of the elements of SQ, as defined by Danah Zohar, a thought leader in this area.[1]

Checklist for Spiritual Quotient (SQ)

What is your SQ? Use the following checklist to find out.

I know and understand my deepest motives.

I have a high level of self-awareness.

I am responsive to my 'deep' self and needs.

I am able to overcome difficulties.

I stand up for what I believe in, even when this means I am in the minority.

I can work against convention.

I am open to experience.

I have a marked tendency to ask the 'why?' or 'what if?' questions to seek 'fundamental' answers.

I am spiritual about religion and death.

I have a high level of personal integrity and honesty.

I am flexible and actively adapt.

I am inspired by vision and values.

I bring higher vision and values to others and inspire them to use them.

I can face and use suffering.

I see the connections between diverse things.

Spiritual resilience

Being spiritually resilient involves having a sense of belonging, purpose and meaning in your work and life and living authentically by your values. This and the following chapter examine these three intertwined aspects, with a particular focus on how they relate to everyday work activities.

Build connections

As humans we are social animals who need to belong to a community of some type. Studies have shown that those with strong

social networks are happiest. Our deepest fear is being discon-
nected from our tribe. While Twitter, MSN, Facebook and
MySpace have opened up instantaneous international communication, they have not necessarily instilled the sense of belonging
we crave.

Building community connections is an important part of
building stability and resilience for us all, especially when we are
children. Good relationships with close family, friends and others
are important. If we accept and offer support to those we care
about this strengthens resilience further.

Within workplaces we can foster this connectiveness through
support and kindness, as explored in Chapter 7. We can also
enhance cohesion by encouraging internal and external network-
ing and ensuring informal time for building relationships.

Create a sense of meaning and purpose in your work

Developing a strong professional identity and sense of meaning
and purpose in our work enhances both our job satisfaction and
sense of fulfilment.

When we talk about employment that contributes to the
greater good we often use the words 'calling' or 'vocation'. Jobs
such as chaplains, charity workers and health professionals come
immediately to mind.

Researchers have discovered, however, that any job can
become a calling, and any calling can become a job. One study
found that among a group of hospital cleaners, some simply saw
their job as cleaning rooms, while others saw it as more meaningful. The latter group of cleaners saw themselves as being a
critical part of the patient's healing process. Investigations found
that these cleaners took on extra tasks such as cheering up
patients and anticipating the needs of medical staff. In essence,
they saw their role as more of a calling than just performing
cleaning tasks.

BOUNCE-BACK ACTIVITY

Creating meaning in your job

Reflecting on the work you do consider these three questions:

▍ How can you increase the sense of meaning and value in your work and promote this in others?

▍ What can you do to relate your job to a higher purpose or goal?

▍ What changes would you need to make to your thoughts or actions to make this shift?

If this is not achievable what could you get involved in outside of work that would give your life more purpose?

If you feel your work does not offer a meaningful purpose you might consider voluntary work. Research into the legal profession, for example, has found that rates of stress and depression are high, with around 11% of lawyers contemplating suicide monthly.[2] Active involvement in pro-bono work, with its corresponding sense of adding value, was found to increase personal wellbeing. As discussed in Chapter 4, a lost sense of meaning at work can be a symptom of burnout.

Develop a vision

A frequently used approach to establishing purpose and meaning in workplaces is the development of an organisation vision. In essence, this is a statement that defines a realistic, credible and attractive future for the organisation. Its purpose is to inspire members to achieve a level of excellence through providing purpose and direction in the work, as well as a sense of what makes an organisation unique. For example, the Salvation Army states theirs is 'a growing, loving community of people dynamically living God's mission in a broken World'.

BOUNCE-BACK ACTIVITY

Developing a career vision

What are the activities you most enjoy doing?

What three things must you do daily to feel fulfilled in your work?

What is your ideal working environment and hours?

What are your core values at work?

What are your personal strengths?

In crafting the vision statement itself follow these guidelines:

▌ Summarise it clearly and simply, writing in first person.

▌ Phrase it in positive language, articulating what you want to do or become, not what you do not want.

▌ Ensure it is consistent and in balance with what you want in your personal life.

To have impact, the vision needs to be believable and realistic, as otherwise it can create cynicism and disengagement rather than shared energy and purpose. It is not uncommon for employees to deride their organisation's vision when what is said is quite different from what they experience.

While the focus at work is often on the organisational vision, you can also develop a personal one relating to your work. A personal career vision statement is a brief description of what you want to focus on, what you want to accomplish, and who you want to become in your work. It is a way to focus your energy, actions, behaviours and decisions towards the career direction you would like. People will sometimes write this on their application when applying for jobs.

Guidelines for developing a personal career vision

Your career vision statement is a concise summary touching on what you want to focus on and become in your working life. This can range from a simple goal such as 'My goal is to become the leading researcher internationally in cuttlefish breeding' to a very personal statement that also reflects your strengths and values. Many advocate that the more personal it is the greater its power as a motivator.

If you see the value in developing a personal career vision then the Bounce Back activity on the previous page will help guide your thoughts. Remember that your vision will continue to change and evolve as you gain insights about yourself and what you want out of your working life. Some examples that may help you crystallise your thought are listed in the box below, Examples of Career Vision Statements.

Examples of Career Vision Statements

My vision is to use my creativity, people skills and commitment to quality to become a respected leader in the Australian food industry, revitalising the way food is produced and marketed, making healthier products to help people live better lives.

My vision is use my intelligence, curiosity and love of learning to earn my degree and become the kind of teacher who changes the lives of students for the better, educating them not only about history, but about the joys and meaning of life.

My vision is to express my perseverance and business savvy by establishing a leading-edge IT business that ensures my customers always get the best, by staying on top of industry trends and creating unique services. The ability to work from anywhere will mean I can travel frequently and have flexible working hours.

My vision is to become an inspirational finance officer within this company by proving my determination and expertise to the managers I work with while gaining the respect of my co-workers through my integrity, strategic capability and commitment to hard work.

Chapter 8: Tips for achieving purpose and meaning at work

▌ Avoid the affluenza trap. Reject the pursuit of enduring happiness.

▌ Know and develop your spiritual quotient.

▌ Increase your connectiveness with others in your personal and working life. Give and receive support.

▌ Create a sense of meaning and purpose in your work. Connect what you do to something bigger and assist others to do the same.

▌ Develop a personal career vision to guide and motivate you.

chapter 9

Living in balance: More on getting the soul right

Achieve work–life balance

The Greeks got it right. Besides inventing, art, science, maths, philosophy and drama, they sang, danced, feasted, played games and told silly stories. To enjoy the riches of life you need to be lateral not spiral.

Ros Miles

Achieving work–life balance is a frequent topic of discussion in lounges, canteens and boardrooms. Human resource staff promote it as part of an 'attraction and retention strategy', while busy managers and staff ponder ways to create more balance in their lives.

As with happiness, this focus on balance has become almost another pursuit of the holy grail, spurring an industry of lifestyle coaches and advisers.

The concept itself is relatively new, having been generated from the discontent of increasing numbers of women entering full-time employment and quickly realising that the superwoman image is not only unrealistic but also undesirable. The earlier cry of 'You can have it all' has become 'You can have it!' Younger generations who have seen the price paid by working parents have also added a voice to this desire for balance, as has the disillusionment with materialism and the increasing need for spiritual growth outlined earlier in Chapter 8.

As a result of this, organisations are experiencing greater demand for flexibility through compressed hours, working from home, rostered days off, and the ability to access banking and other facilities at work. Realistically though, many of these approaches do not actually decrease workload, rather they increase our sense of control over our job. In turn, this feeling of more control decreases our sense that work is dominating our life. However, if our expectation is that flexibility allows us to do it all, it can set us up to fail. With too many balls in the air there will inevitably be some on the ground at any one time.

An over-emphasis on decreasing or modifying working hours often deflects from the true meaning of balance — the capacity to be able to do the things that matter most to us. Many people work long hours but continue to thrive because what they are doing is of fundamental importance to them and there is nothing else they would rather do. This means that balance is not so much a work–home time issue as a values issue.

In assessing your life balance ask yourself the question: 'Are you creating time for the things that matter?' Try out the exercises on the next page to discover your assessment of your current work-life balance.

Life balance is very individualistic. What portrays balance for you may not appeal to your co-workers. Achieving it is also difficult, as many of the demands placed on us, such as family commitments, are non-negotiable. These demands also change throughout our lives as our responsibilities shift and interest in investment in our career changes. Surprisingly though, some sense of balance can be achieved, despite our commitments, by

> **BOUNCE-BACK ACTIVITY**
>
> ## Investing in life's domains
>
> A balanced life means investing in all aspects of your life including:
>
> ▋ work and career
>
> ▋ personal development and growth
>
> ▋ relationships (social, family, romantic)
>
> ▋ health and fitness
>
> ▋ finances
>
> ▋ recreation and leisure.
>
> Rate from 1–10, (where 1 is low and 10 is high), your satisfaction with each of these domains of your life and with your life overall.
>
> Once you have rated each domain, write one or two sentences that sum up your current situation in each of these aspects of your life.
>
> Next choose one or two areas that you would like to invest more in and develop an action plan for these.
>
> Remember that the priority you choose to place on each of these domains will shift overtime according to life's circumstances and your past achievements.

creating space in our daily routines for activities we enjoy — playing sport, pursuing a creative endeavour, volunteering or simply having time out to do something for ourselves. If it is important to you and you put boundaries around the time you need to do it, you are achieving more of a balanced life.

Other obstacles to balance outside of personal responsibilities can be far less tangible and relate more to guilt or entrenched beliefs or standards about what we *should* do rather than what we *have* to do. Part of our modern-day stress is trying to have it all, do it all and be it all. We believe we should have a good job, earn a good income, and own a nice car and house. We should be a perfect wife or husband, mother or father, son or daughter and be there for our children, boss, family and team members. The *shoulds* in our lives may not only come between us and what we want to do, but may also hinder our self-acceptance and peace of mind. Working on letting go of the 'shoulds' can be a lifelong journey.

Many workplaces profess to offer work–life balance while their culture — that is, the unwritten rules of how things operate — promotes quite different expectations. Managers who work long hours without holidays are role modelling what is expected to get ahead in an organisation. As happens with parenting, staff will do what they see being done, not what they are told to do.

Within the team there may also be practices that counteract beliefs that you can take advantage of flexibility arrangements. Routine early or late meetings, weekend travel schedules and limited work breaks during the day are just some examples. These group norms can overshadow formal organisational protocols and processes and often do. It seems that despite copious research on the need and value of balance, there is still a predominant view that extended hours at the workplace are what makes a productive worker.

Live your values

> *Try not to become a man of success but rather try to become a man of value.*
>
> Albert Einstein

Closely connected to spending time on the things that matter most to us is an understanding of our core values. In general terms, a value is an important and enduring personal belief or ideal about what is good or desirable and what is not. Values exert major influence on our behaviour and serve as broad guidelines in all that we do. They act like a personal compass to indicate what direction to take in situations we encounter.

Living your values is simply being true to yourself and not compromising what is important to you. What are your core values and how do they influence your work and life? Some people develop a simple 'litmus test' to guide their decision-making at work. Here are some examples:

- If this decision appeared on the front page of the newspaper tomorrow would I be happy for my friends and family to read about it?

- Is it legal, is it moral and would I be happy to be associated with this?

- If I met this person walking down the street in the future would they still acknowledge me?

- If I look back on this months or years from now would I feel proud of how I responded?

These reflections offer a flavour of what you might include in your own 'litmus test'.

When our buttons are pressed, as described in Chapter 6, it's likely that the incident relates to a value that is important to us. Perhaps our integrity or honesty has been called into question or our expectation of equity and fairness has been breached.

Organisational values

The extent to which we enjoy our work will depend on compatibility with the unwritten values of the organisation we work for. If we highly value compassion and honesty, for example, we will find it difficult to thrive in an environment driven more by profit than caring for customers and their needs. While the purpose of companies will always be to make profit, organisations such as The Body Shop have shown that this can still be achieved with a strong moral consciousness.

In recent years organisations have attempted to harness the power of values through establishing shared values and using these to guide staff behaviour and promote organisational identity and brand. Businesses now commonly promote their values both through their literature and visually in the environment. In theory, a set of shared values decreases the need for extensive procedures and protocols as they provide a compass for decision-making.

Typical values advocated by organisations include integrity, respect, courage, honesty, compassion, loyalty, creativity, innovation, accountability, challenge, connection, support, fun, harmony, excellence, bravery, quality, trust and tolerance.

Trends in society towards increased social and moral consciousness have also prompted organisations to use altruistic values as a differentiator in the marketplace. Many companies now integrate elements of corporate social responsibility (termed 'CSR') into their strategic plan. In essence this is a commitment to behave ethically and contribute to economic development while enhancing the quality of life for the broader community. Sustainability is often part of this, with a focus on preserving the environment and natural resources for future generations.

Contemporary models of leadership, such as transformational and authentic leadership, also highlight the importance of values. Effective leaders are seen as holding vision and integrity while prompting shared purpose.

The difficulty comes in translating organisational values into behaviours on the ground. If what happens on a day-to-day basis is in contradiction to what is promoted by leaders' values, as in the case of a vision, can become a source of cynicism or derision. A lack of transparency when, for example, the promoted value is trust, demonstrates the actual versus articulated culture. If leaders micro-manage when the espoused value is creativity, the inconsistency becomes an issue. This means that the use of values can be highly motivating or de-motivating as they are at the core of what we believe in and what drives us.

Take a strengths approach

We learn from our mistakes. [Conventional wisdom]

There is a growing emphasis in recent times on playing to our strengths as a means of enhancing life satisfaction.

In workplaces we have traditionally emphasised identifying and developing weaknesses. Performance reviews and other job assessments typically focus on our 'development areas' — that is, what we need to work on and improve. Supervisors, to their chagrin, often spend far more time supporting workers in their deficiencies than leveraging from their capabilities. While we need to acknowledge scope for improvement in performance, the attention on this often detracts from understanding and working with what we are good at.

A new school of thought from positive psychology is the need to focus more on identifying and capitalising on our strengths. We all have different talents by virtue of our skills, knowledge, personality and special aptitudes. Discovering these and using them daily helps build job satisfaction and effectiveness. In contrast to the myth that we grow most in our areas of weakness we do in fact become more of who we are. At best we can move from bad to okay in tasks we do not shine in while we can bloom in our areas of strength.

As an example, if we are a conceptual and creative thinker who enjoys flexibility and an unstructured approach to work, a time management course to get us using highly structured work processes will not reap benefits. It is better to work with our strength of big picture thinking, innovation and overseeing multiple projects. This is not to say that we do not need a degree of organisation when we are at work, rather that we need to create an environment where the type of organisation required is not highly structured and strengths can be capitalised on.

The first step in taking a strengths approach is to determine where your strengths actually lie. Only you are qualified to identify what these are, as a core requirement is that you feel personally strong when you engage in them. As an example, others may comment that you are good at negotiating contracts, but if doing this does not make you feel strong it is not actually a core strength.

Psychologist Marcus Buckingham[1] advises that in identifying strengths you need to consider if:

• you feel successful and effective when you do it
• you are drawn to doing it and look forward to it
• you are focused when engaged in it and actively interested in it
• you feel fulfilled and authentic when you've done it.

This task is not as simple as it looks and will require consideration and reflection.

Once you have identified your strengths, the challenge is then to create opportunities to use them in everyday activities. If you are a leader you should also recognise and nurture these in others. This element is seen as integral to effective leadership today. For example, transformational leadership, a well-researched and popular model advocates considering the different needs, abilities and aspirations of team members and helping them to develop their strengths.

Use your signature strengths

Closely related to the work of Buckingham is the concept of signature strengths developed by psychologist Martin Seligman.[2] Philosophers since Aristotle have focused on virtue and what constitutes a good life. After extensively researching this, Seligman has proposed that one way of creating meaning in your life, at work and at home, is knowing and regularly employing your signature strengths.

These strengths have been derived from investigation into traits that meet the criteria of being malleable and valued in their own right (that is, not just a means to another end), in almost every culture.

Seligman found a surprising convergence across cultures and generations in his research. While there was disagreement on the details, six core virtues were found to be universal, which included:

- wisdom and knowledge
- courage
- love and humanity
- justice
- temperance
- spirituality and transcendence.

These virtues were then developed into the 24 signature strengths listed in the box on the following page, Seligman's 24 Signature Strengths. As you read through these you will find that some strengths are more characteristic of you than others. Identify the top five that you most associate with. Some of them, such as kindness and curiosity, you can display frequently, while others, such as valour, may be displayed only if you have the opportunity.

The premise is that we will have a more satisfying and authentic life if we know, use and build on our core signature strengths. In a similar way to Buckingham, Seligman advocates that instead of devoting our energies to correcting our weaknesses we should build on our strengths.

Seligman's 24 Signature Strengths

Wisdom and knowledge

Curiosity/interest in the world

Love of learning

Judgment/critical thinking/open-mindedness

Ingenuity/originality/practical intelligence

Social intelligence/personal intelligence/emotional intelligence

Perspective

Courage

Valour and bravery

Perseverance/industry/diligence

Integrity/genuineness/honesty

Humanity and love

Kindness and generosity

Loving and allowing oneself to be loved

Justice

Citizenship/duty/teamwork/loyalty

Fairness and equity

Leadership

Temperance

Self-control

Prudence

Humility and modesty

Transcendence

Appreciation of beauty and excellence

Gratitude

Hope/optimism/future-mindedness

Spirituality

Forgiveness and mercy

Humour

Zest/passion/enthusiasm

BOUNCE-BACK ACTIVITY

Determining your signature strengths

Compete the free on-line questionnaire at www.authentichappiness.org to determine your signature strengths. Note those you score highest on. Take notice also of your lowest-rated strengths as these are also a source of useful information about yourself.

Chapter 9: Tips for living in balance

▮ Achieve work–life balance by making time for the things that matter most to you.

▮ Invest in all of your life domains to build a sense of balance.

▮ Know and live your values. Encourage this in others, including your team.

▮ Recognise and build on your core strengths.

▮ Understand and use your signature strengths on a daily basis where possible.

chapter 10

Sustaining resilience: Continuing on the journey

Staying on track

Making a personal resolution to build resilience is one thing, keeping to the plan can be quite a different story. If changing behaviour was easy we would all be looking and acting according to our ideals. We'd be slim, fit, healthy and living the life of our dreams. This final chapter explores realistic ways of making and sustaining the changes you aspire to.

As a starting point, it is useful to reinforce the essential ingredients we need to reach our personal goals. There are four main requirements, including:

- a personal belief that you are capable of doing what you want to do
- the autonomy to make the decision to do it
- advice and support on how to do it
- self-motivation and a desire to change.

Assuming that earlier chapters have sufficiently equipped you with the first three of these ingredients, this chapter explores tips on how to stay motivated and driven towards your goal of increased resilience in one or more of the four domains.

Just get started

> *The journey of a thousand miles begins with one step.*
>
> Lao Tzu

The longer you delay starting to make changes in your life the less likely they will happen. Whenever you are contemplating doing something different it is best to commence straight away. This means that if any of the ideas in this book appeal to you, try them out as soon as you can and then notice and build on your progress. If you have been reading these chapters over a prolonged period you should have already started making gains. Building resilience is an active not an intellectual journey and cannot be attained by reading a book.

Start with the end in mind

Be clear about your vision in relation to each of your goals. What exactly will it look like if you achieve what you are setting out to do? How would you personally determine you have made a shift, and what would others around you notice? Having clarity about the outcome will not only be more motivating but will help you determine your level of success.

If the change you want to make is less tangible and is more concerned with changing the frequency or intensity of behaviour, a scaling approach as described below may be more effective. As an example, changing work–life balance may be an action with a final observable outcome, while becoming more mindful is an internalised shift without visible outcomes. The former may lend well to visualising the end result, while the latter may not.

Relating back to the resilience model in Chapter 1, remember that you will need to invest in each of the four areas of resilience, although not necessarily equally.

Include shifts in your existing routine

When it comes to changing how we think or act, it is helpful to keep changes consistent with our current schedules. Recall the last time you enthusiastically decided to lose weight, relax more, or improve your time management. How long did it take long before your good intentions became lost in daily routines and projects?

Lost intentions are even more likely if we are already overwhelmed, as additional goals just add to our pressure levels. In these circumstances it is easy to quickly relegate an idea to the 'too hard basket'. This is especially the case in workplaces where there is often limited discretionary time available to concentrate on additional tasks.

We know that change is more sustainable when it is embedded as a small shift in our daily routines. This is not difficult when it comes to resilience-building, as many of the suggestions in this book do not actually take time — they just demand a disciplined change in the way you think or act.

As an example, if you would like to enhance physical resilience you can gradually integrate small shifts into your daily work routine, such as regular walk-and-talk meetings, blocking out diary time for self-care, keeping nutritious snacks close by or leaving on time at least twice a week. In contrast, joining a gym and attempting to exercise at 6 am when you are not a morning person is doomed to fail.

With ambitious goals that will take time and effort to achieve, you will need to determine how you will break the goal down into the small manageable steps required for sustainability.

Sir Edmund Hilary, reflecting on his quest to reach the summit of Everest, reinforced the power of small doable steps.

He said: 'We had very simple equipment and very primitive climbing techniques. The only thing we really knew how to do well was carving one step after the other into the snow. In all humility I can say that we were champions in simply shaping and preparing the next step in the snow or ice, which then got us one step closer to our goal.'

Small incremental steps can still have a big impact, as a number of small shifts in behaviour on different levels, especially on a team, can create considerable overall change.

Another useful idea is to consider five simple things you can do each day to build resilience. In the same way that we routinely clean our teeth for oral health we can also invest consistently in our mental health. The list could include simple actions such as expressing appreciation, practising mindfulness or reframing at least one negative thought. What you choose does not matter as much as your increased conscious investment in your resilience. If each person in a team or family engages in this the cumulative effect can make a big difference.

Pay attention to progress

Paying attention to the progress you have already made can both build motivation and offer a perception of success you can celebrate and build on.

One way of actively recognising the small shifts you have made is by asking yourself periodically 'What is better?' This will focus your attention on what is already working well and will steer you in the right direction. When you search for the small differences that signify progress you may notice that there is more proof around than you expected. This can build personal confidence in your progress. The bounce-back activity on the next page is a useful demonstration of this.

The 'Me Diary' idea shared in Chapter 5 is another tangible way of recording how far you have come.

BOUNCE-BACK ACTIVITY

Actively notice change

Take a blank piece of paper and record at least 25 things that have become better for you since you began reading this book.

While identifying that number may seem challenging, you may find when you start to reflect the list may be even longer.

Another useful tool is scaling, as described in Chapter 3. This involves rating where you are on a scale of 1–10 and determining:

- what it would look like if you moved up one rating and what the next steps would be to do so
- what you have done to reach the level you already rate yourself at and how you can leverage off these ideas and approaches
- whether you have been persistent in searching for what already exists in relation to your goals.

An example of this is contained in the bounce-back activity at the end of this chapter. You will see that scaling can be used as a demonstration of progress and is also a useful way to break down less tangible goals into smaller steps.

Work within your scope of influence

In a similar way to needing personal autonomy to implement change, you also need to develop goals that are predominantly within your control. Goals that are dependent on the actions or reactions of others are not motivating. Such thinking is also counter to the key strategy for building cognitive resilience in Chapter 2; that is, focus on where you have influence and can make a difference. Remember too that for things to change, first we must change.

Persist despite obstacles

I'll be back.

The Terminator

Obstacles will invariably appear along the path to your goal. Anticipating these and pre-determining the strategies you will deploy helps. Identifying, for example, how you might tackle colleagues who may unconsciously sabotage your optimism or drain your positive energy will decrease the perceived size of the blockage when and if it arises.

It also helps to be patient and recognise that breaking long-held routines and patterns takes time. Anticipating roadblocks and accepting these as part of life decreases the inclination to give up straight away.

Another perspective-shifting technique is to also acknowledge that not going backwards when unexpected temporary setbacks occur is actually progress. As an example, if you are working on being more positive and you become ill, not regressing to your previous level of pessimism is progress. If you are working towards life-balance and you have a change in role with a temporary workload increase, not regressing to old habits is also progress.

Keep your options open

Multiple strategies also help us stay persistent. As described in the discussions of Hope theory in Chapter 3, we need a number of pathways to our goal. What may start as a promising option may not work for you, and having another to experiment with will increase your opportunity of achieving successful change. Having one path and stopping when it is blocked displays a lack of 'staying power'.

Employ your tool-kit of coping responses for the varying setbacks or stressors you will encounter. All situations are different and the same approach will not always bear fruit. In some circumstances, for example, you can concentrate on generating different solutions to a problem, in others you may need to build your energy reserves or be less emotionally reactive. A repertoire of responses from all elements of the resilience model is beneficial.

Ensure support

Sharing your goals with others promotes personal motivation for two reasons. First, you have publicly stated your intentions and will not want to look like you have failed; second, others can act as a personal coach to spur you on. As an extra incentive it will also mean you will have somebody else to celebrate your successes with. Choose somebody who you know will encourage and believe in you.

Look out for role models

Watching how others successfully handle situations you also encounter is useful. Look around for role models, recognising that you will need more than one, as what works for another person may not fit with your personality. We all cope differently and need to tailor our actions according to our personal style and specific circumstances. Multiple role models will increase your response repertoire. You may have a colleague who seems to stay calm under pressure, or a manager who is always positive and approachable.

Mentally rehearse change

As explored in earlier discussions on building cognitive resilience we know that mentally rehearsing our goals will make them more likely to come to fruition. Using the Storyboard Technique in Chapter 2 is one useful way to do this.

Understand the cycle of change

We can sometimes fall into the trap of thinking of change as being an 'all or nothing' venture. We try something for a while and when it doesn't work out as planned we give up. Diet and exercise regimes are examples that readily come to mind.

Specialists in behaviour change, Proshaska and Di-Clemente, hold a contrary view, suggesting that the process is cyclical, involving a pattern of adoption, maintenance, relapse and re-adoption over time.[1] Their model, as portrayed in Figure 6, identifies five stages that we need to move through to achieve successful change. If we use getting physically fit as an example, the five stages are as follows:

Stage 1 — Pre-contemplation: When you are considering exercising more frequently in the foreseeable future.

Stage 2 — Contemplation: When you are aware a problem exists, such as being overweight or unhealthy, and are seriously considering doing something about it.

Stage 3 — Preparation: When you are committed to taking action and have engaged in some minor physical activities with limited success.

Stage 4 — Action: When you have changed your behaviour and kept up an exercise routine for less than a few months.

Stage 5 — Maintenance: When exercise is part of your lifestyle and you work to prevent relapse and consolidate the gains made in Stage 4.

It's likely that we will move back and forth between the five stages for some time, experiencing one or more periods of relapse at earlier stages before moving through the to the action stage and eventually, maintenance.

If we think about change as cyclical, we can expect it to involve both progress and relapse. As an example, a setback in your optimism following a difficult experience does not mean you have reverted to your previous pessimistic state, it simply means you have moved back a step in the cycle from action to preparation.

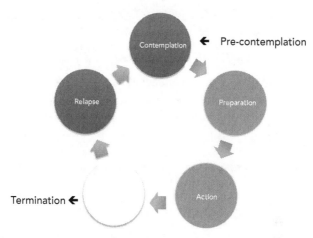

Figure 6
The Prochaska-Di Clemente Cycle of Change.

Given we live in an environment with fluctuating positive and negative influences, linear movements upwards will always be challenging. As described earlier, progress can simply involve not going backwards when there has been a lot of extra pressure on you.

The most important implication of the cyclical progress though, is understanding that each stage requires a different mindset. For example, we may need more evidence of the need for change in the pre-contemplation stage, while more support and embedding into daily routines is useful during the preparation stage. Using the appropriate thinking for each stage better sustains progress. Surprisingly, people who initiate change without outside help are just as successful as those who have expert assistance if they intuitively identify the strategies they need at each phase of the change cycle.

BOUNCE-BACK ACTIVITY

Applying the change cycle

Identify one of your goals in building personal resilience. Using Prochaska and Di-Clementes' model, identify where you are in the change process. Determine and employ the strategies that best fit with this stage.

Resilience: A continual work in progress

Building resilience, as with any personal development, is a continual journey. One way in which you can return to this book and review your progress and possibilities for the next step in your journey is through using scaling. The bounce-back activity on the opposite page outlines how you can do this.

You will also find that the activities and ideas will resonate differently for you at different stages of your life. This means that returning to chapters at a later date may further add value.

Sharing techniques within your team is another way of adding momentum to the journey, as each of your colleagues will find different techniques useful. Even a small number of shifts by team members can cumulatively create a major change in group dynamics and resilience. Alternatively, if you do not want to engage with your team in any of the activities suggested you can make an impact simply by role modelling — especially if you are in a position of leadership or influence.

BOUNCE-BACK ACTIVITY

Assessing progress and future possibilities

On a scale from 1–10, indicate where you stand in relation to each of the aspects of resilience.

Cognitive resilience

1   5   10

Physical resilience

1   5   10

Emotional resilience

1   5   10

Spiritual resilience

1   5   10

For each of the scales, what are one or two things that will make you notice that you have moved up 1 point from your current rating? How will your work colleagues notice that you have moved up 1 point?

A final note

Resilience is the key to surviving and thriving in an increasingly complex world. Developing physical endurance, emotional balance, mental toughness and meaning and purpose for life's inevitable setbacks is challenging, yet achievable. Modelling it as a leader, colleague, parent or friend, as well as assisting others in the journey, builds community resilience and capability well beyond what we can achieve alone.

Best wishes with your personal journey in falling down many times, but bouncing back each time.

Endnotes

Chapter 1: Exploring resilience

1 Statistics on mental illness are as reported by the Mental Health Council of Australia in 2010.

2 The developmental model of resilience, as shown in Figure 1, was developed by the author.

3 'Positive psychology' is the umbrella term used to describe the psychological movement that focuses on fostering happiness and wellbeing and helping people be the best they can be. For an overview see *Positive Psychology in Practice* (2004) by Alex Linley and Stephen Joseph, published by John Wiley & Sons.

Chapter 2: Reframing problems

1 The Eisenhower Principle originates from the work practices of US President Dwight David Eisenhower, who prioritised and delegated his work according to its urgency and importance.

2 John Nicholls (2001). The Ti-Mandi window: A time-management tool for managers. *Industrial and Commercial Training, 33*(3), 104–109.

3 A useful resource with a variety of visualisation exercises for personal change is *Visualisation for Change* (1988) by Patrick Fanning, published by New Harbinger.

Chapter 3: Embracing life

1   Further information on creating solution-focused questions can be found in texts on solution-focused coaching, such as *Brief Coaching for Lasting Solutions* (2005) by Insoo Kim Berg and Peter Szabo, published by W.W. Norton.

2   A useful overview of appreciative inquiry is contained in *Appreciative Inquiry Handbook* (2005), by David Cooperrider, Diana Whitney and Jacqueline Stavros, published by Crown Custom Publishing.

3   Edward De Bono details his six thinking hats approach to problem solving in his book *Six Thinking Hats* (1990), published by Penguin.

4   Ishikawa diagrams, also called fishbone diagrams or cause-and-effect diagrams, are diagrams that show the causes of a certain event. Causes are usually grouped into major categories such as people, materials and the environment. The model is commonly used for problem-solving in workplaces.

5   For more on Wiseman's principles of luck and how to apply them read *The Luck Factor* (2003) by Richard Wiseman, published by Random House.

6   Martin Seligmann's definitive book on optimism is *Learned Optimism* (1993), published by Random House.

7   Polyanna was a child heroine created by American writer Eleanor Porter. The term is used to describe an excessively or blindly optimistic person.

8   Rick Snyder is widely recognised as the leader in Hope theory. A useful reference on this area is *Handbook of Hope: Theory, Measures and Applications* (2000), published by Academic Press.

9   Disputing and reframing self-talk derives from cognitive behavioural therapy. For more detailed examples of applying this techniques see *Change Your Thinking* (2006) by Sarah Edelman, published by the Australian Broadcasting Corporation.

10 Thought defusion is commonly used within Acceptance and Commitment Therapy, a therapeutic technique that has become very popular in recent years. A useful text to explore this further is *The Happiness Trap* (2007), by Russ Harris, published by Exisle Publishing.

Chapter 4: Investing in self-care

1   The Job Demands-Resources (JD-R) model was developed by Professor Arnold Bakker and can be used to predict employee burnout and engagement. See www.arnoldbakker.com for more details.

2 The concept of calm and tense energy is contained in *Executive EQ* (1997) by Robert Cooper and Ayman Sawaf, published by Orion Business Books, London.

Chapter 5: Rejuvenating the body

1 Mihaly Csikszentmihalyi's seminal work on flow is *Flow: The Psychology of Optimal Experience* (1990), published by Harper and Row.

Chapter 6: Channeling emotional energy

1 There are a plethora of books on emotional intelligence. The text accredited with popularising the concept was *Emotional Intelligence* (1996), by Daniel Goleman, published by Bloomsbury.

2 The term 'emotional labour' was first defined by the sociologist Arlie Hochschild' who saw it as managing feelings to create 'a public facial and bodily display'. She describes jobs involving emotional labour as those:
   • requiring face-to-face or voice-to-voice contact with the public
   • requiring the worker to produce an emotional state in another person
   • allowing employees to exercise a degree of control over their emotional activities.

3 Extensive research into the 'dark-side' of personality and assessment of this has been conducted by US psychologist Robert Hogan.

Chapter 7: Creating positivity

1 A comprehensive text on positivity and its benefits is *Positivity* (2009), by Barbara Fredrickson, published by Crown.

2 Many studies on gratitude have been conducted by Michael McCullough of University of Miami and Robert Emmons from the University of California.

3 For more information on Allan Luk's study and the concept of 'helper's high' see his website at www.allanluks.com

4 The tendency to catch and feel emotions that are similar to others is known as 'emotional contagion'. One view is that we have a tendency to automatically mimic and synchronize facial expressions, vocalisations, postures, and movements with others. Consequently we then experience similar emotions.

5 The FISH Philosophy was created by John Christensen after being inspired by employees at Seattle's Pike Place Fish Market. Noticing they were animated and happy in their work he arrived at four key concepts that need to be integrated into all workplaces.

6   For more information on the 'Being a good teammate' exercise see *Primer in Positive Psychology* (2006), by Christopher Peterson, published by Oxford University Press.

7   To explore the concept of savouring further, see *Savoring: A New Model of Positive Experience* (2007), by Fred Bryant and Joseph Veroff, published by Lawrence Erlbaum Associates.

Chapter 8: Achieving purpose and meaning

1   For more on spiritual intelligence, read *Spiritual Intelligence. The Ultimate Intelligence* (2001), by Danah Zohar and Ian Marshall, published by Bloomsbury Publishing.

2   A study by Professor Ian Hickie from the Brain and Mind Institute showed that the legal profession has the highest amount of depression among any profession in Australia. The study, the largest-ever survey of legal practitioners and students in Australia, found that almost a third of solicitors and one in five barristers suffer depression. The results support earlier findings that the incidence of depression in the legal profession is four times higher than in the general population. Lawyers consistently rank first in surveys on depression, with one study finding that 11% of lawyers contemplate suicide every month.

Chapter 9: Living in balance

1   Marcus Buckingham has written and co-written a number of books on strengths including *First, Break All the Rules* (1999), *Now, Discover Your Strengths* (2001), *The One Thing You Need to Know* (2005), *Go Put Your Strengths to Work* (2007) and *The Truth About You* (2008).

2   Martin Seligman's work on virtues and signature strengths is contained in the book *Authentic Happiness* (2002), published by Random House.

Chapter 10: Sustaining resilience

1   For more information about processes of change, read the chapter by James Proshaska and Carlo Di Clemente, 'Towards a Comprehensive Model of Change', in *Treating Addictive Behaviours: Processes of Change* (1986) edited by William Miller and Nick Heather, published by Plenum Press.